The Ancient Words of Wisdom

The Ancient Words of Wisdom

Universal messages from Spirit

Scribed by Nita Jane

First published 2024
Copyright © Nita Jane 2024
The moral rights of the author have been asserted.

All rights are reserved, except as permitted under the Australian Copyright Act 1968 (for example, fair dealing for the purposes of study, research, criticism or review). No part of this book may be reproduced, stored in a retrieval system, communicated or transmitted in any form or by any means without prior written permission from the author.

What is written in these pages has been channelled through Spirit and my higher self; the words are not directed nor have implications toward any specific individuals. I have no time to think or prepare for what I am to write. It is an account of what may or may not have taken place. There are no references or evidence to show that these events may or may not have occurred. They are merely sensed and felt by the writer and directed by the Universal energy, God, Elohim, Spirit, or the Divine, whatever you may call the higher power. These terms are used interchangeably throughout the book, and you can also substitute your own preferred name for your higher power in their place if you wish.

Edited by Ignite & Write Publishing
Cover design and typeset by BookPOD

ISBN: 978-1-7635652-0-3 (pbk) ISBN: 978-1-7635652-1-0 (e-book)

 A catalogue record for this book is available from the National Library of Australia

Dedication

To my dear Millennial, Generation X, Generation Z, and Generation Alpha children,

The day you fall in love with yourself is the day you have found God within.

You are the misunderstood and forgotten era. *You* are the ancient words of wisdom. You always were and always will be.

When God whispers, we awaken.

Foreword

Lost and unsure of their place in the world, a twelve-year-old child reaches out to The Creator through text messages. The child uses tech prayer as they are too shy to verbally express themselves openly for fear that others will overhear their plea from God.

Unaware that The Creator will respond, the child is surprised to have questions answered. The barrier that the child had previously put up has now been torn down as the child listens to guidance and becomes more relaxed while communicating. The text exchange may be fictitious but take from it what you will. These words are not my own but have been dictated through me to you and for you.

The Ancient Words of Wisdom

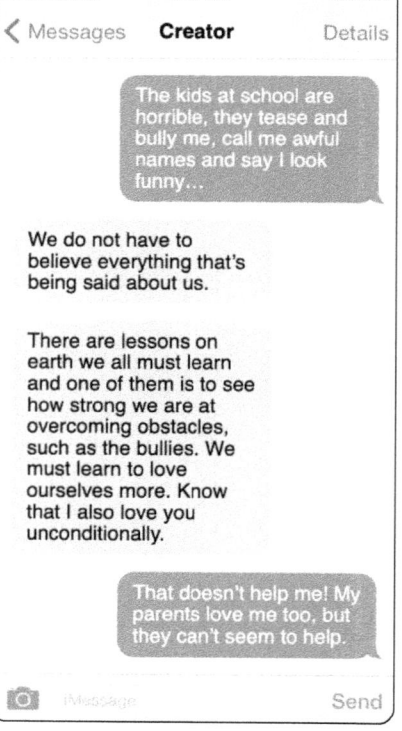

Scribed by Nita Jane

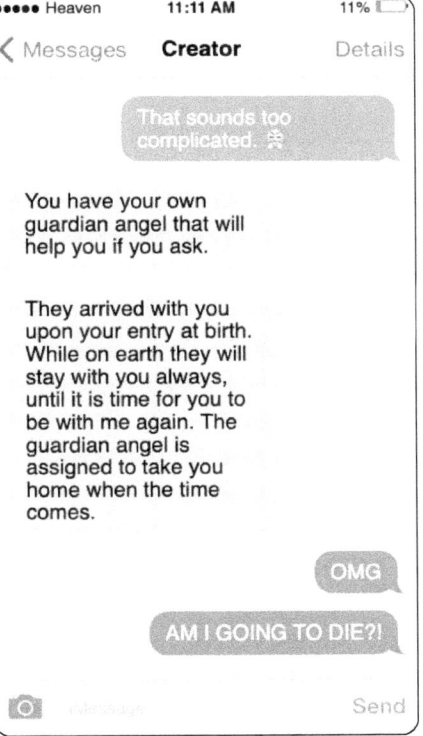

The Ancient Words of Wisdom

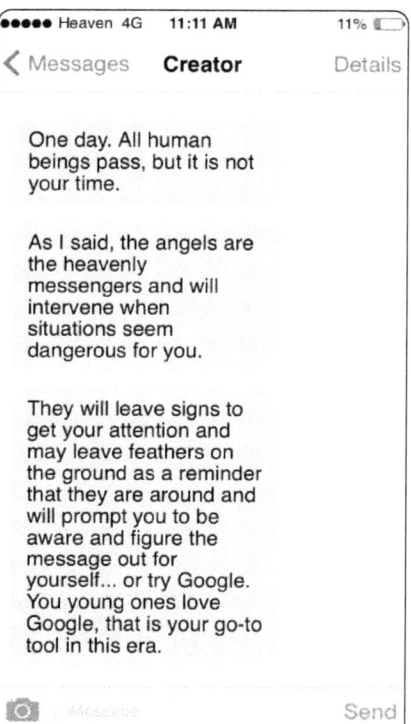

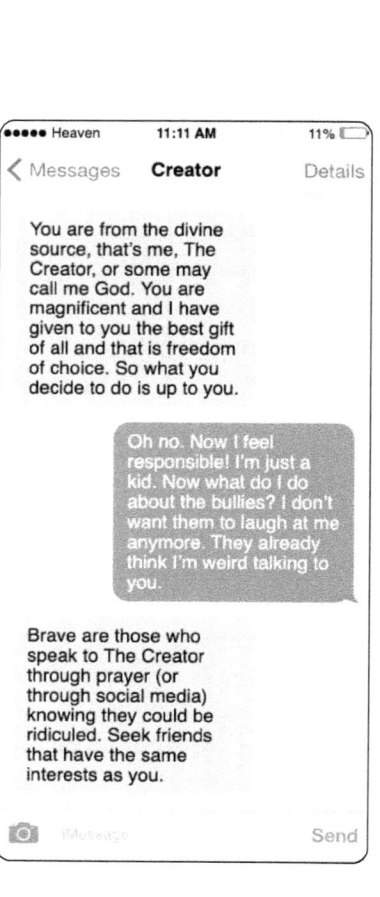

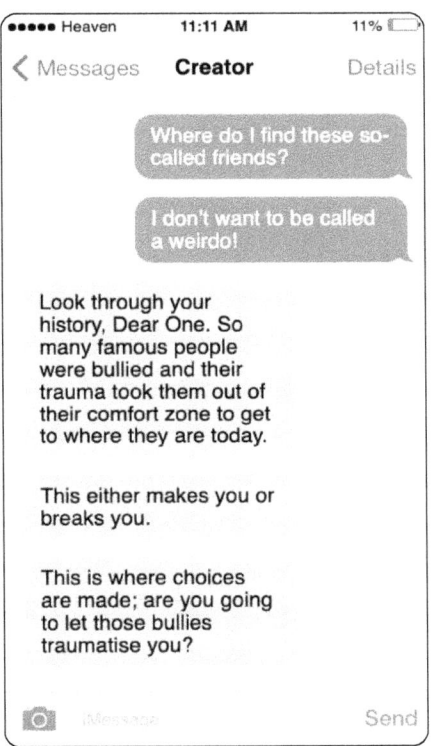

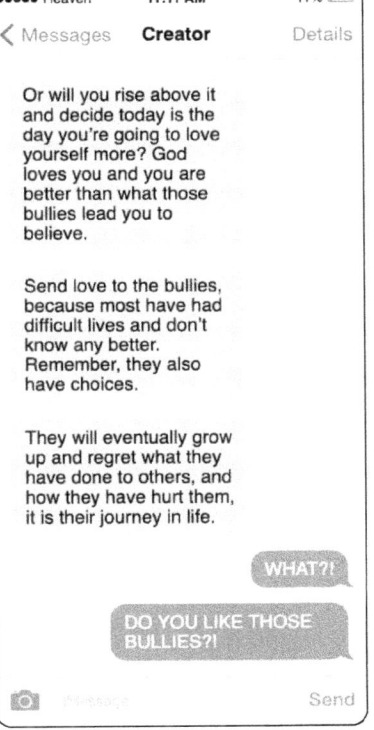

The Ancient Words of Wisdom

Scribed by Nita Jane

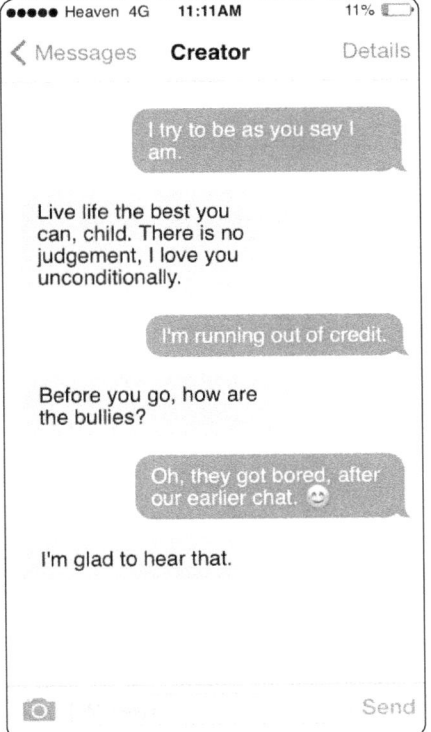

The Ancient Words of Wisdom

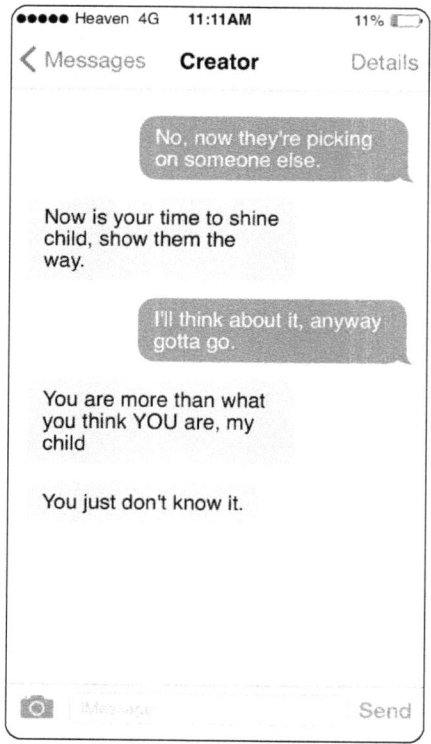

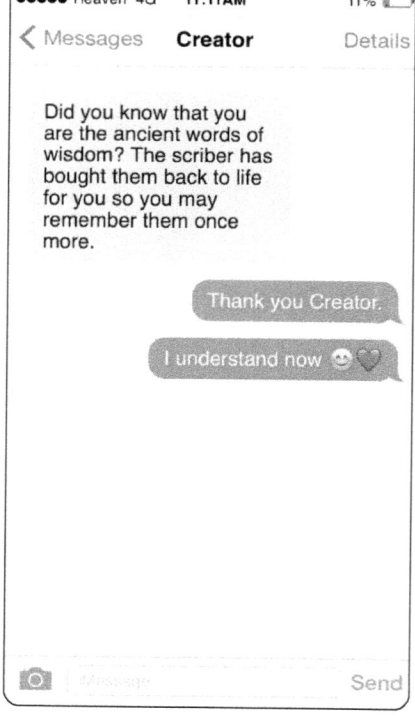

A Note for Caregivers

Dear adults and caretakers of our next generation,

Children today are advanced souls, and technology is their legacy. They have been born with talents and gifts way beyond their years. However, they are unable to control the innate power they have inherited.

We continue to compare our children to the 1960s Baby Boomers, the children who played outside late until the streetlights came on. The children who drank water straight from the hose. Today is a different era and a different timeline. Let us move on from this reference and gain another perspective on helping rather than ridiculing.

Let us try a different approach, a new way of being for these children. Let's be honest, we do not understand them very well. It is almost like they come from a different planet, but it is more like a different frequency and vibration that we, as adults, do not fully comprehend. It is out of our scope.

As their earthly Guardians, how can we understand these advanced little beings? There is so much debate on how these children have been raised. How do we capture their attention? What platforms do we use? How do we get the next generation of children to read these words of ancient wisdom (or any book, for that matter) so they are inspired? How will they be open to guidance, and what guidance can we provide for them at school and in society?

Not everyone is a genius and wants to be a doctor, lawyer or scientist. There are too many expectations placed on children to comply with today's standards. Children and young people are beginning to become afraid for their future and hide in their parents' shadows, still living in the family home well after twenty years of age or older. Whether it is due to economic times or lack of social skills and other factors, these young people seem to be anxious about the world around them, as if it poses a threat.

The school system is not equipped to accommodate new-age children and young teens. We must help them to become well-adjusted and balanced human beings first before trying to mould them into something they are not (they will not stand for it anyway, hence the rebellion most have now). Having confidence and knowing who they are should be a priority before all else. It starts in the home.

The new era of social media has taken over the airspace with TikTok, Facebook, Instagram, and all other platforms and websites that have now become inundated with followers. This is all the children of this time know. Virtual reality has become part of their norm. So, where do we find a balance between reality and virtual? How do we change things around so that the children of this era are not so addicted?

Many children want to become TikTok influencers because that is what their whole life revolves around. The lure of easy money comes with stressful expectations to achieve. Unrealistic personalities with numerous alterations to their body appear to be able to inspire the younger generation with their multi-million-dollar existence. For some, this is an unrealistic goal. These 'influencers' seem to be walking advertisement billboards and human beings who are no longer recognisable.

The next generation will find comfort in themselves once they have found the Divine within. We have to ask ourselves as adults, 'How are we going

Scribed by Nita Jane

to change our attitude toward these children in order to help them?' For they are the next generation of leaders, and we cannot allow them to fall into despair but rather uplift their life force.

These beautiful children have ideas and are creative little beings; however, they lack the practicality and implementation to carry forth their ideas. I am not talking about all of the new-age children, only a fraction.

Like a lattice of tapestry and artistry, many faces are woven lifetime after lifetime, creating the perfect human being. The gift of a thousand lives we have breathed, with so much joy and laughter as well as suffering.

We cling like vines to a tree, hanging on for stability to be nurtured, like a child holding onto a parent's leg while learning to walk, for fear they will fall. The roots of the tree are steadfast and stoic and will dig deep into the ground with all its might and energy, holding on until it is either uprooted by a mighty storm or felled from its foundations.

Our existence has become like that tree we have held onto; our foundations so firm it has become detrimental to our health. We find ourselves unable to let go easily for fear of failure or triggering past traumas, which carry on through to our next lifetime. We are unaware that these traumas exist; we only know they hurt us physically, mentally and emotionally, and we are unable to rid the demons that keep creeping up on us. Spiritually, we are exhausted and do not know where to turn to overcome such baggage. All we want to do is go home, but we don't know where home is. We just want to stop the pain we feel about life and how to live it.

As a mother and grandmother, I observe the struggle the younger generation has endured, physically, mentally and spiritually, and it upsets me to know that we, as adults, sit idly by and watch as our children and grandchildren are bullied and ridiculed by adults who are supposed to love, support and guide them through life.

The Ancient Words of Wisdom

Please do not take for granted what you already have. I ask that the light protect the *Ancient Words of Wisdom* so they may speak to all who need them. The world is a place of uncertainty, and there is hope for the young in these pages. These words are for them. These words are simple and easy to understand, and we must create a platform for the younger generation to reach out to them so they feel they are being nurtured and not left behind. The children are caught up in an era where their parents don't know why they are the way they are and cannot find an answer to the many questions they have.

Children are intelligent little beings born into a society of technology. We must nurture them, for they are our future, and they need balance in their lives to keep them grounded. They have created for themselves a culture of destruction, and if that can be turned around, we will have a society of future leaders in their own right and wonderful human beings.

I am tired of humanity putting them down and saying they are spoilt brats. No, they just know what they want, and it sure isn't the B.S. they have been raised with, that's for sure. They don't need dictators; they want someone to *show* them – to be role models. There is a whole generation of people who missed out on being nurtured properly. We have no clue how to raise the next generation. That is why these children are lost; caregivers have pushed them aside and sat them in front of technology to babysit them while they themselves play video games or surf the internet or Facebook. Caregivers today need re-educating on how to raise this new generation in order for them to be well-balanced individuals. No judgement here.

We need to be more loving and caring toward these children so we can gain their trust. Adults must teach children how to love themselves by showing them *how*. When they see you love yourself and not putting yourself down or having destructive thoughts, they can follow that example. How do you expect children to behave if you are doing the opposite of what you want them to do? No wonder they're so confused.

Scribed by Nita Jane

We as parents, grandparents and society as a whole need to change our attitude because we can't handle these non-compliant, outspoken children. It is good to voice your opinion in a positive way. But please be a positive influence and allow these children to have their say and listen to them respectfully before you react. When we can do that, these children will grow up to love themselves and know exactly where they are headed and how they're going to get there.

They are the generation that everyone has forgotten about or doesn't want to know because they are known as the 'entitled ones'. Well, who done this to them? They didn't do it to themselves, that's for sure. They are bright, beautiful, loving individuals who need to be taught to love themselves first so they can love everyone else. Let us show them that this is possible, and let us be the mantle of change for them. Let us love them more and try to understand them, and hopefully, the schooling system will change to allow that to happen. Because once you have a fully functioning child who loves themselves and others in turn, you will have a well-balanced adult who is able to function to their full potential.

Hopefully, you will start recreating yourself now that you know it will help your children evolve into better human beings. We are looking for change and peaceful times ahead. Start looking at life from a different perspective and questioning everything and anything that you're not sure about.

Nurture your child. Be a mentor, Guardian and a pillar of strength for them. No child is broken or needs fixing; they just need someone to listen to their plight and help them to understand. Most children have become the teachers of their parents. The children today are solution solvers. Therefore, we do not need to place upon them old paradigms and belief systems, as traditional education systems continue to do. I believe, to indoctrinate them into our way of thinking is a criminal act.

The Ancient Words of Wisdom

I look forward to the day that all of this is implemented and comes to life. Our children need us to support them right now, for they are the generation that is struggling the most. Let's make a change.

I do not claim to be the perfect parent or grandparent. I am still learning from past experiences and mistakes. As I reread the message above it is a clear reminder – something I can reflect on and to take note for myself, as I evolve to make positive changes in my own life. I take inspiration from the young ones today, for they allow me to become more creative in the way I approach and communicate with them.

To be a caregiver to our precious little treasures is both challenging and rewarding at the same time. To all those who have chosen this journey with God's little miracles, believe me, it is not an easy task. May the blessings be!

Much love,

Nita Jane

Contents

Foreword vii
A Note for Caregivers xv
Introduction 1
The Ancient Words 9
    Acceptance 9
    Addiction 10
    Akashic Records 12
    Alternative healing 13
    Angels 15
    Anunnaki 18
    Aquarian Age 19
    Arcturians 21
    Attachment 21
    Awakening 22
    Balance 24
    Beauty 25
    Belonging 26
    Bible 27
    Body 28
    Bravery 32
    Breathe 33

Celestial beings ... 33
Change ... 36
Channelling ... 36
Clarity ... 38
Climate change ... 39
Closure ... 42
Collective ... 43
Communication ... 44
Compassion ... 46
Complete ... 47
Compliment ... 49
Confidence ... 49
Connection ... 50
Creativity ... 51
Crop circles ... 52
Crystals ... 53
Cycles ... 55
Death and rebirth ... 59
Dear traveller ... 59
Dedication ... 60
Depression ... 61
Destiny ... 64
Direction ... 65
Disasters ... 67
Disease ... 70
Dream ... 71

Empathy 72
Emotions 73
Empowerment 73
Energy 74
Energy healing 75
Eternity 78
Evolution 79
Expansion 79
Expression 80
Extraterrestrials 82
Fairies 86
Faith 87
Family 89
Fear 91
Feminine energy 92
Fight or flight 95
Flow 96
Forgiveness 96
Foundation 97
Freedom 98
Free will 99
Full moon 101
Future 103
Generations 104
Geniuses 104
Give and receive 105

Gratitude	106
Growth	108
Happiness	108
Harvest moon	109
Heaven	111
Higher realm	111
Higher self	112
Identity	114
Illumination	115
Inspiration	116
Intuition	117
Jesus	118
Journey	122
Judgement	123
Kailash Mansarovar	123
Kundalini	125
Learning	128
Lemurian	130
Light beings	132
Light codes	133
Love	135
Luck	137
Manifest	137
Masters	138
Meaning of life	139
Meditative consciousness	141

Memories 142

Mind 143

Mindfulness 144

Miracles 145

Mother Earth (Gaia) 145

Music 147

New beginnings 148

Nourishment 149

Numerology 151

Old soul 153

Parallel Universe 154

Partnerships 156

Patterns 157

Peace 158

Perfection 159

Pictures 161

Power to act 162

Pure consciousness 162

Purpose 165

Pyramids 168

Reflection 170

Regression 171

Regret 173

Resources 174

Respect 175

Responsibility 176

Sacrifice 178
Self-belief 178
Self-improvement 180
Simplicity 183
Soul or spirit? 184
Soul groups 186
Soul travel 187
Sound 188
Spiritual encounters 189
Spiritual enhancement 191
Suffering 193
Survival of mankind 193
Synchronicity 196
The Creator's gift to the world 196
The goddess 198
Time 198
Together 200
Transformation 201
Trees 202
Truth 203
Twin flames 205
Unique 206
Universal awareness 207
Universal energy 209
Validation 210
Value 211

Vibration 212

Vision 213

Water 214

Wisdom 215

Work 216

Acknowledgments 218

About the author 220

Resources 222

Introduction

Ko au ko koe, ko koe, ko au –
I am you and you are me

To my dear Generation X (born 1965 – 1980), Millennial (born 1981–1996), Generation Z (born 1997–2012) and Generation Alpha (born 2010–2025) children.

The *Ancient Words of Wisdom* have resurfaced once again during this century to remind you of who you truly are. For so long, you have been misunderstood and shunned by a society that does not understand your boldness to go where others will not.

You are faced with so much uncertainty, ridiculed as selfish, privileged and unruly – the list goes on. In amongst all of the noise, you have forgotten your true purpose on Earth. You fight for your right to be heard but, alas, are not understood.

You've come back, old soul, to right the wrongs of your past. Failure to stop the war and the destruction caused by your last incarnation on Earth will be different this time around. You are the ancients who were forced to obey and become submissive and conditioned by corrupt leaders of their time and to be executed for your truth in the past. You will not let that happen again, this time around the sun. Dare to step out of line, dare to say your piece, speak your mind and dare to get punished for it.

The past, present and future interweave as one. Use the right tools of self-love, self-esteem and care for the environment; and most of all believe in self and know the reason and purpose for coming to Earth. Be comfortable with who you are, that is the key to a well-balanced being. There is no need to be hostile in order to be heard.

Modern society has turned everyone into zombies who are reliant on television, the internet and all media technology. Innovation is great, but put in the wrong hands, it becomes a monster that turns on itself. It is time to switch off and wake up.

Remember, Dear One, the *Ancient Words of Wisdom* were entrusted to you all many centuries ago. They were written in many forms and scripts to support and reflect on who you were through many lifetimes. Hieroglyphics on walls and paintings depict the first communication etched in stone and animal skin, creating written documentation of those who lived before on Earth.

The Divine has chosen this as the time to remind humanity of these ancient words, for they ring as true today as they did when they were first written. It is no accident that you hold this book in your hands right now; these words are ready to speak to your soul and guide you on your path.

Creating *The Ancient Words of Wisdom*

Spiritual encounters are not unusual for me. I was blessed with this gift as a child, and I come from an ancestry of seers and healers. With my six decades on Earth, I have been a seer and Reiki healer, doing all I can to follow my faith and live with love and intention.

But in 2019, I experienced a spiritual encounter unlike anything I had experienced before. While seated at my dining room table, I decided to read tarot cards for a family member as guidance for the day. We as a family do this often. However, this time, it was different. As I read the cards, I asked a question, and in doing so, I heard my own voice reply with an answer. When I spoke this out loud to my family members, they confirmed it to be true.

How did I know that? Although the voice was my own, the information received was not something I would ever have had knowledge of myself. So, I asked, "Who are you?"

The voice responded, "We are The Collective, and we come from the galactic federation of light".

This response frightened me. Although I was used to spiritual encounters, this was different. I remember someone telling me that when entities or guides enter into your space, you need to ask them whether they come in the Christ light and in the name of Jesus. So, of course, I asked that very question three times. A very soft voice replied, "Do not be afraid, Dear One, for we come from the cosmos, as do you. You have sat and scribed with us for many lifetimes before this one, and it is not new for you, for we are one."

My human side became curious, but the soul side of who I am knew it was okay, so I was reassured and felt calm and right with it all. I was uncertain for a long time before I trusted what felt right for me and was confident that nothing would hurt me or interfere with my life.

The more questions I asked, the more relaxed I became. I realised the celestial Messengers were not there to take possession of my body and soul but have connected with me to help spread their messages to those who seek to know answers about themselves and how the universal energy affects them.

The Collective, as they are called, have so much love and patience for me. No matter what kind of ridiculous questions I ask, they come back with love and support and remind me that I always have free choice. If I chose to relinquish all contact with them, they would be willing to wait until I was ready and step aside until then.

I have never been an articulate person, nor had a wide vocabulary of descriptive language to draw on in order to write, and I tend to waffle too much. But when I connect with Spirit, I am amazed at how the words seem to dance across the pages and take shape into a story without any effort. It is clear that I am merely taking dictation.

If I do not understand what they are trying to convey, my higher self shows me a scenario – it's like watching a movie. The concept is shown to me, so I understand what the message is. The words also flow swiftly, and it is up to me to try and interpret as much as I can and to keep up with the flow, although nowadays, it is not necessary – I finally get it! I now feel like I am reconnecting with long-lost relatives and want to talk all night. I feel blessed every day to connect.

My body now prepares itself to take on the higher frequency and vibration needed to take on such a task. We are one now, and I am whole and complete. What I know for sure is the information that I receive is as real as the nose on my face. I have witnessed so many miracles and astounding revelations from the higher consciousness. The information flows through the higher self into the pen that connects with the journal. With precision, love pours forth from the words because they are sacred and come from the purest realms.

The Ancient Words of Wisdom is a guide that will be shared with the world. Together, we have written so many breathtaking words. I am reminded how much God loves us and wants so much for us every time I read them. The Creator reminds us that we can be more and do more because we are part of the *all*. I feel blessed every day to be in the presence of such wonderful and pure Guardians full of unconditional love. I no longer fear or have judgement on anything or anyone. They have helped me overcome a lot of my insecurities. I am human and have negative thoughts sometimes. However, the majority of these have now disappeared due to being free to express myself openly.

I am honoured to sit with the ancients and scribe in order to bring the words alive again and share them with the world. No longer will they sit in the dark and gather dust. For the year is right for them to be bought back into the light. Persecution in this era does not exist. We are free to express our beliefs. Bringing *The Ancient Words of Wisdom* to light will give anyone searching for enlightenment the opportunity to read their words. It has been foretold that the ancient words of wisdom will be shared again, for the next generation needs to read and hear them. They are simple messages with cryptic meanings, which you will interpret in your own way and fill your life with things to think about.

How to read *The Ancient Words of Wisdom*

What is written in these pages has been channelled through Spirit and my higher self; the words are not directed nor have implications toward any specific individuals. I have no time to think or prepare for what I am to write. It is an account of what may or may not have taken place. There are no references or evidence to show that these events may or may not have occurred. They are merely sensed and felt by the writer and directed by the Universal energy, God, Elohim or the Divine, whatever you may call the higher power. These terms are used interchangeably throughout the book, and you can also substitute your own preferred name for your higher power in their place if you wish to.

There are many references to 'going home' in this book. This is a way of describing what happens to our eternal soul once our bodies cease to exist on Earth. Depending on what you believe, going home could mean taking your place in Heaven, being guided to the next realm or having the opportunity to find your place in the mortal world once more in another form.

People ask me how I know what to write when I connect to the Universe. The truthful answer is that I do not know until the pen hits the paper. While scribing the messages for this book, there were times when the messages were ready to flow through fully formed and others when I remained a blank canvas until I asked a question, any question. For this reason, you will see some messages are spoken directly to you, others are a conversation between myself and the Divine, and others are written in my voice and include my thoughts and experiences. No matter how they are presented, the messages are for you.

The Ancient Words of Wisdom is not a novel; it provides guidelines to elevate and help you to understand yourself. Human beings are facing a crisis at the moment. Fighting against themselves, loneliness has become the fundamental overarching paradigm at this stage. If human beings only knew they were not alone and never had been, they would live a more fruitful life instead of one of misery and longing. For all have choices in life. One must examine oneself thoroughly to understand what one's soul and spirit are lacking and proceed to fulfil the need without fear, judgement or criticism. Just do it!

As you know, we are not given a manual for life, we have to figure this out for ourselves. I am reminded every time I read these words how much The Creator loves us and wants so much for us. I remember that we can be more and do more because we are part of the *all*. I feel blessed every day to be in such a wonderful presence of pure, unconditional love.

Scribed by Nita Jane

Each time you pick up this book, you will experience it differently. Even if you read the same passage, different elements of the message will sit in your heart or ring true. It may be something you paid no attention to the first time around, but the time was right for you to really sit with those words. Divine intervention is perfect. Allow the knowledge you have gained to guide you to where you need to go. I would have loved to have found something like this many years ago while I was searching for answers to simple spiritual practices.

If this is not working for you, there will be another pathway to follow. The *Ancient Words of Wisdom* are from the realms of the Universe. Therefore, they are sacred and need to be treated with respect and honour. They come from vaults of the masters, who have scribed these very words before, so all who seek the truth will read and become inspired and reassured by what they already know deep within themselves.

I am in awe of the volume of information that Spirit have shared with me. The words give me something to think about all the time and they are presented among these pages in a way that allows you to feel into their power. Open to a page at random or choose a heading that speaks to you or sparks your curiosity. Either way, you will find what you are looking for at any given moment.

May these words bring you much joy, love and happiness. Let the words express themselves openly and honestly to your heart. Awaken and listen, feel the words as they resonate within your soul for they have been gifted by The Creator, so be at peace and may unconditional love shroud you in bliss.

Love and light,

Nita Jane

The Ancient Words

Acceptance

We all want to feel accepted, one way or another. It is, without a doubt, one of the most emotional times when we feel we have no place or we do not fit in anywhere.

We stand alone and watch from afar as everyone is placed in their circle of friends and colleagues. We only wish we could fit in, but we don't. We are not the norm and never will be. We are only accepted because of the gifts and talents The Creator bestowed upon us. No one fully understands us, and we are considered weird and wonderful. So, how do we separate ourselves from our God-given gifts so we can be accepted? Why would we want to do that? You were given these gifts for a reason, so you have no need to separate yourself at all.

We have begun to accept ourselves, and that is enough. We walk alone to do God's work, and that is more important than trying to fit in. The human side weeps alone, but the spiritual side rejoices, knowing we will never be alone. The masters guide us, the Angels hold us, and we are loved unconditionally. That is all we need to remember.

> *"Indeed, it is due to our choosing*
> *to accept or reject that we do not*
> *see the true nature of things."*
> – Sosan

Addiction

Scribe: Why is the world full of drug addicts at the moment, and how can we stop it?

This is a human choice. What can we do? It pains us to watch humans destroy themselves. Dear One, it is free will. We can whisper in your ear, and we can send signs to help. However, we cannot take over someone's choice. Strong is the human who battles mental illness. We are so proud to know that they will work through the trauma and hurt, no matter what it takes. They search until they find the answer to their prayer, "Please Lord, take this from me".

The drugs take out many human beings and also alter their whole perspective on life. This is what they signed up for before entering the Earth as a baby. However, they are being replaced by new souls on a daily basis. These are the beautiful Indigo and Crystal children – the light that leads the way for all mankind. This is the new DNA that will soon make up a new generation of all human beings. The shift will be for the better, Dear One. You will not be here to see it, but you and others like you will be back, reincarnated as these children.

Scribe: Why do I need to come back?

To help humanity. By then, you would have rid yourself of all the emotional baggage that still weighs you down today. Dear One, deal with your past and release what holds you back. Be comfortable with who and what you are: the kind soul who we have chosen to come with us on our journey. We invite you to visit with us in the cosmos, the galaxy.

You all have access to the same resources, and you are more than capable. Imagine going through an addiction; you are definitely not alone, although you think you are. As far as depression goes, there are many out there who have this debilitating affliction. So, what we are saying is that many are alone in their struggles to stay alive, and yet we are supposed to be more caring about those who cannot help themselves. We are more common than we think. Humans are humans, and regardless of what class of people you come from – poverty or wealth – we are the same. Rather, human beings move through different stages in life depending on what their mission is on Earth. From rags to riches and vice versa, it is quite easy to do; it is how one copes with the issues that one faces and the attitudes during the experience.

What habits do you want to break? Alcohol addiction, cigarettes, food? Whatever it is, you've got to figure out how you got there in the first place. It's a weakness that triggers multiple sensations in the body. The mind again starts playing games with you, and you fall for it every time. It's a sad boat to be on with the tidal waves of emotions involved. We make lame excuses for our addictions, and we blame others for making us this way. Poor you! You must follow your own path, not the path of whoever you looked up to as an alcoholic or out of loyalty. Believe me, that's not a life; it's a waste of one's life.

Sometimes, you think you can change others and their addictions – to rescue them from themselves. You can't. They have to want to change themselves. If you are in a poor relationship, the only thing you can change is yourself and whether you stay or not. You cannot change the other person, no matter how much you love them. You think you can; that's why humans stay in bad relationships because they think *one day it will happen, they will change*. Don't waste your breath because there are more important things out there for you to do. You're not giving up on them; you are becoming your authentic self. In doing so, your shift may just be the wake-up call the person needs to begin their own healing journey.

Break loose from the bondage that holds you.

Akashic Records

Scribe: Can you please tell me about the Akashic Records?

One is living in an infinite world with no beginning and no end. Visions of lifetimes move like pages flickering in the wind, so are the many lifetimes that man has lived. Those lifetimes are recorded for The Creator to examine. The information gathered is for one purpose: to improve all our lifetimes.

The deeds are all in the Akashic Records and are all available for everyone to access. If you would like to find out more about yourself, the library is open for business.

Scribe: Is there a process that one must follow?

Think of the process in a meditative state without thought or meaning while being present and aware. Now ask the question, depending on what facts you are asking about yourself.

Within the meditation, envision the biggest library of floating shelves you can imagine or whatever you envision them to look like. Ask the Guardians, using your full name and date of birth, about the information you would like to access. In an instant, the information will fall from the shelf, which will show you anything you want to know about your past, present and future.

Thank the librarians for assisting you. They are the special Angels whose sole purpose is to take care of the Akashic Records. The music that comes from the halls is so beautiful; it is unlike anything you have ever heard before. Dear One, seek your records if you must. You are where you are supposed to be for a reason. You have been very patient, and we understand it has been a long process for you, but we need you to be ready to bring your mind, body and soul into alignment. There was a time when all human beings were able to access anything in the spirit realm; it was not for just a few of you.

For some human beings, it has become difficult because, over time, they have strayed from the true Source and allowed different doctrines to dictate their way of thinking and doing. Human beings have become dependent on others to access the spirit world for them; they are the light workers or the awakened ones. All humans have the same capabilities. It is in oneself to seek the unknown or what they deem as unreachable.

Beloved, we are humbled by your curiosity and love for mankind. Remember why you are here, know your purpose is to create what you want and know that all things are possible. Chase away the negative thoughts that do not serve you. Nothing is complicated unless you choose it to be. We know your body is adapting to changes, allow this to happen naturally.

Change your beliefs. Change your thoughts. No one is making you believe anything. You came to the Earth as a high vibrational being. There is amnesia when you get to Earth because you could not hold the higher frequency in a 3D consciousness. What was designed for you is all stored in the Akashic Record.

> *My wish for you is to find your purpose before you leave the Earth, otherwise you will be back to fulfil the same quest over and over again.*

Alternative healing

The beautiful colours of the chakras – purple, blue, orange, green, violet, turquoise, amber and white – are a combination of all colours. The colours vibrate to different sounds and frequencies within the body. The chakra practitioner chooses the right crystal that resonates with a particular ailment within the patient and places it on the body along the meridian. The stone vibrates to the specific frequency of the body temple. Some stones are not compatible with some patients; therefore, it is crucial to try and align the chakras perfectly in order to heal the body of their ailments. Kinesiology will help to recognise the correct crystal. One size does not fit all. We are the same. However, our soul developments differ in all of us. Therefore, use the correct tools if you want to be a chakra balancer.

Human beings are evolving, and so is their body makeup. Now more than ever before, young ones are coming through with totally different DNA systems, so drop the old way of healing – it is of no use now. No rituals are required. Guidance is needed more for the young ones because although they are advanced, they have no idea what they are dealing with, hence why many chose to leave and go home rather than ride the waves of life. There is no leader young people can follow, and they are quite lost.

Too much technology has interfered with the human anatomy and is causing havoc in the body. Digital devices like television, mobile phones and tablets need to be used in moderation to lessen the effects of exposure.

Spirit has realised the need to shut down communication briefly soon to allow the young some space. Ideally, they will start to realise the internet is not everything. What exists will be replaced with better-quality communication services.

Technology also distracts humans from pursuing their purpose in life. We only get one chance in this life, so why not make the most of it, challenge yourself, and see how far you can proceed?

You must push forward and ask yourself, *why am I here?* Go and find out what drives you and makes you happy. Find people who have the same interests as you do. Meeting others like yourself challenges the emotions, which is a good thing. In reality, they are a reflection of who or what you may or may not want to be. It may make you a stronger individual when you are faced with the reality of someone just like you. Some people may not see themselves in other people or deny that they have the same attributes, and that is okay. To see yourself in someone else could be the inspiration you need to step forward to challenge yourself to accept things you cannot change.

Accept all challenges – you are more than capable.

Angels

You make me laugh; you make me cry. You are the rays of sunshine that glow in the dark. You are the warm hugs that I feel everywhere; you are the Angels I feel in my hair. You mean everything to me, and I am so blessed to have you near.

When I am afraid, you whisper in my ear. You let me know that you are right there and that you will never leave me. Who am I? Your Guardian Angel of course, and as time continues, the body starts to age, but the soul continues on. So, take good care of that body of yours, and you will find yourself living the dream. No more will you suffer from ailments such as fatigue; stress less and go with your instincts.

Scribe: Do people see Angels?

Yes, they do.

Scribe: Who are they, and how did they come about?

They come from the realm of The Creator. They are the Messengers.

Scribe: Are you able to tell me something about the Angels that have not been mentioned anywhere else please?

Human beings are given a Guardian Angel at birth. This Angel reincarnates with you and never leaves you. Human beings all have the ability to see them at a physical level, but of course, some are more tuned in than others. Very few have been able to witness the full extent of what an Angel is capable of. Lorna Byrnes, author of *Angels in My Hair*, claims this is so. We do not deny or confirm that she can. We only know that, for some reason, she has been taken to the spirit world a few times and has sat in their presence. The love that resides in her is far beyond a normal human being capability. She *is* love and radiates it so.

Angels cannot interfere with human choices, but they can whisper or show the humans signs. Take note, Dear One, listen. There are many books written solely about Angels, and they are also referenced in religious texts from the *Bible* to the *Quran*.

As you know, Angels were created to serve human beings. They are capable of transforming themselves into human form to help the person through difficult times, but this is very rare. They can bring dreams to human beings in their sleep state or even while awake, this is called day dreaming.

History dictates and claims Angels are indeed real. Angels are soldiers ready to fight for human beings. If you are to envision an army willing to do anything to keep peace and harmony, this is what they do. The Creator has put in place so many support systems for His children; some disregard them altogether. We try to make life exciting so that you prefer to stay and experience it. Whether good or bad, remember it is your sole purpose to go through it all. It is for you to find and create another scenario to get out of a particular cycle. The Angels are there to help protect you. Call on them; that is what they are designed for.

We cannot answer your question fully because we are aware that the words written will be for all human beings to read. We do not want to jeopardise anything that may cause harm to the human and the Angels as well. They are radiant beings and do not have negative attributes at all. They radiate full love, compassion and all that The Creator has.

Scribe: To be touched by the Angels is nothing like I have ever felt before. It is a mother's caress with the warm light breeze as they shift your hair. They whisper, "Be happy; we are here to protect you. We love you always and want what's best for you. We are the Messengers sent by the Divine. We watch over you and drop our feathers in your path to let you know that we are around. We came with you as you entered Earth's atmosphere and will leave with you on your departure homebound. While you are here, we are your guides and will never leave you. You must ask us to help you when you need us, for we cannot intervene unless we find it necessary, for we know you can figure most things out on your own. We are real, as real as the nose upon your face. Although most cannot see us, we are here. We are peace-loving energy, and we vibrate at a high frequency. Never be afraid, for when we walk in, the dark disappears. We love you eternally in this life and the next."

Your Guardian Angel is always with you. Ask, and ye shall receive. You will never be alone, so remember to call on the Angels when you need them and thank them.

> *Angels above me, Angels below.*
> *Angels surround and protect*
> *me wherever I go.*

Anunnaki

Scribe: Who were the Anunnaki?

Evidence dictates that they were a superior race, one who created man and interbred with humans, using some for enslaved people and others to rule and conquer. The DNA was changed to encapsulate the rulers' blue bloodlines. Enslaved people helped to extract gold from mines in Africa. The gold was used for ingesting because it has the potential to enhance human anatomy within the system, which gives it magical powers. Dear One, I am The Creator of all. At this point in time, humans are not ready for anything that will tip the scales.

Humans can speculate what they want about the ancient tablets, which illustrate the use of the gold dust. Evidence that the past inhabitants have left behind is not all accurate. Too many humans have their own theories and tend to speculate; they think that what they have found in ruins is fact. Not all facts found are to be true. Artefacts that have been excavated point to different theories. No one can get this right. Everyone wants to be the first to discover an ancient civilisation. The archaeologists who have found the correct information regarding the Anunnaki have left this Earth some years ago. While the discovery they made was correct in many ways, this was hidden from the everyday person. To know the truth was certain death of a whole nation of humans, or it would have resulted in a whole civilisation wiped out with the technology you have today.

Gold dust was ingested as it was believed to have spiritual purification, rejuvenation and/or medical capabilities. Historical records show that gold as an ingredient originated at least 5000 years ago and was consumed in certain areas of Asia, Africa and Europe. It was said that the properties it contained varied from region to region and even changed over time as well.

It is still being ingested today by the elite and, whoever can afford edible gold flakes added to their food. However, modern research suggests that edible gold flakes do not have any health benefits, and it is more a way of introducing greater extravagance in meals.

You are loved, now and forever.

Aquarian Age

Time to rise up and take your place in the order of things. Take a stand in what you believe in. It's all about self-awareness, doing what feels right for you and coming out of the darkness into a new way of thinking.

Scribe: What do you mean?

If the paradigm of life for you was very strict and you became a meek and mild-mannered child, a trait you have carried through to adulthood, the Age of Aquarian is a time to work through issues and get rid of baggage that does not serve a purpose for you anymore. Find better strategies to lighten the way you think. Forgive yourself for what happened in the past. The past need not interfere with what happens now.

Remarkable human beings were born in the Age of Aquarius, Abraham Lincoln was one. Free thinking individuals who made a difference to your world. It can be so again. Touch somebody today by the way you speak, by the way you think and the way you include others. Human beings love to be part of a group or mean something to someone. It can be a lonely place out there for some. Be kind, loving and thoughtful. A kind gesture and a compliment are all that's needed to uplift those that life has forgotten.

Thinking of others before yourself and taking the time to say, "Hello, I see you". It's all about changing thought patterns and perhaps giving life a go. Moving on from where you are, changing jobs, moving house, getting into something you have never tried before, or staying at one thing and advancing in that particular field or subject. It's about not becoming stagnant and not holding onto old ideas that do not provide essence for you anymore. Moving forward helps to accelerate the serotonin within our body, which sends excitement and wonder to a new adventure. We can become stuck in the chaos of mundane living. Start the fire burning again, release the endorphins, which will help the tired, worn-out winter blues. Life is in your hands, serve it with a big hit!

Bear witness to the thousands that will leave Earth's surface within the next ten years. Right now is the time to get over your fears – the fear of speaking in public; face the fear of not knowing what is next for you. Embrace the light, for we want your love to help us to grow. Feel the warm sun on your back. Know that we will support you, Dear One; know that we can never leave you. Know that we are like the light that flickers in the trees above the canopy of life. We are the moon and the stars. Create a space for yourself; get to know who you truly are. Surround yourself with positive people and events.

Mix more with others, particular people who will be put in your path. You will help each other, whether it be for emotional support or simply to test your experience with that person or groups of people. Being able to cope with someone else's energy, whether that be positive or negative. The challenge, Dear One, is for you to cope with trying to understand how you feel and how you will come out of this experience unscathed.

> *"The way is perfect like vast space where nothing is lacking and nothing is in excess."*
> – Sosan

Arcturians

Scribe: What are the Arcturians?

Beings of the fifth dimension, Christ consciousness, a multi-dimensional field. We currently live in a three-dimensional existence but can function in a fifth-dimensional consciousness. Observance and being five-dimensional allows us freedom. This is the highest aspect of you; while the third dimension keeps you safe, waiting in the same old state, working, coming home, which is everyday living.

Humans experience movement from the third and fourth dimensions and even to the fifth dimension, going in steps to experience all but always coming back to third-dimensional consciousness because your body is of this realm, and you still reside here. The only difference is when you are contacting the higher beings. They are in the fourth or fifth dimensions, and while you can go there, they cannot come to the third dimension because it's a lower frequency or vibration.

Dear One, you are your own unique 'you'. We have told you multiple times that you do not need to seek confirmation from any one shape or form. I understand, but there was no one who could help you to fully take hold of what you were experiencing. Seek those who have gone through the same process.

> *Inspired by Spirit and loved by the Divine, what more could you ask for?*

Attachment

Attachment can affect all human beings in a positive or negative way. An attachment means not having the ability to let go; this also applies to material goods, including houses, cars, etc. Nonsensical items that impede the human being in attaining enlightenment on a spiritual level. If one is solely focused on material wealth, one only has to question why that would be more important. Perhaps you have gone through poverty at one stage in your life and care not ever to go through that again. Still, material attachments are something to hold onto rather than letting go. Society has dictated this to you through generations, and that's all you know. If material goods are what makes you happy, there is no judgement here.

> *We live in a timeless world where nothing is solid; we flow like water.*

Awakening

The blinding lights of hope that shimmer far off in the distance are for all to claim their right to be here on this Earth. Know that you have a mission to fulfil while on this Earth. Do not leave every stone unturned. Witness the awakening of the many when they realise who they truly are.

Masses will awaken to the tune of the Divine within. Be happy, joyful, always laughing at yourself and the silly, quirky things you do. Please. The heart desires the right to sing. The gift of love, the time to give to all the music to hear the Angels that put us here.

Dear One, shake the foundations of expectation and heed not to the outspoken, for they fall foul of their own demise. Concentrate on love and peace, for these two things are the way to eternal bliss. Forget the worldly troubles and embrace the spirit realm, where all is calm and freedom reigns. Fulfil your magical life. From love to eternal being, being you and all of you, from your head to your toes. Your existence does not falter, for you are the master of your own life, so grab hold and don't let go. Go along for the ride, you might like it.

Dear One, you have lived through some harsh times. We want you now to enjoy your life on Earth and be as vibrant as possible. Be eternally happy, live the heck out of life, laugh and love, be healthy and physically fit, and have the ability to captivate the hearts of all who come into contact with you. I see your smiley face and the way you take care of others. It's time to take care of yourself. There will be no more disappointments in your life, only love and understanding. Things are about to change.

Promiscuous, deadly and untruthful, the decline of man is his own making, and the collective force is recommended for the billions to recognise their faults. With love and perseverance, anything is possible. Delight in the ever-changing, embellish in the ever-developing situations, indulge in the love and bask in the God light, like the humans who have not come to pass. Imagine the likelihood of knowing the Universe better than we as humans ever have. Celebrate the possibility that humanity will survive and will elevate to a better and bigger universal state.

When an individual awakens, there is celebration. The human being finally arrives at a conclusion that they are able to see a lot more than they used to. Colour becomes sharp everywhere you look, and fauna and flora come to life. Everything brightens, in my opinion, because that is the spiritual and true essence of the human being having a wonderful experience. I wish for many more people to awaken. We experience emotion, and it becomes difficult to control and work through such an ordeal. Begin to ride the waves and let it take you to where you are supposed to be. Life is not a race. It is supposed to be enjoyed, so go with the flow and let everything happen naturally. When we force an issue, it starts to become unbearably difficult for us. Slow down, think about things clearly. Your aim is a peaceful existence.

When you learn about yourself and your capabilities, you can see life through fresh eyes. You will awaken the ability to see beyond what is already in front of you. Know there is more to you than first thought, experiencing phenomena you cannot explain. Recognise numbers that appear frequently and question why and what they represent. Find answers to many questions about dreams, ET, the galaxy, God, the Divine, *where do I come from*, and *why am I here*? What is my higher purpose in life? Look at the bigger picture, know there is more to life out there and how to live a better life. You start to relate more to animals, the environment, space and time; you are always curious about life and where it might be taking you. Always question relationships with the people in your life, are they supporting you or hindering your walk down the spiritual path? Research to understand where you're going is great; find connections and like-minded people!

Blessed are those who see the kingdom of God within. Awaken to the next level of existence.

Balance

You are considered majestic, a beautiful being. The Creator's miracle. The life He gave to you is a gift, and as with many gifts, you just don't know what you have until they are unwrapped carefully. It is up to you to use your gifts to help others and to know your full potential without ego. Once you recognise your capabilities, you can support others in their search for creativity and natural idealism.

Living a wholesome and happy life is one of the most positive and rewarding ways to live, without fear, anger or hopelessness. Becoming a well-balanced human being is something that we all strive for. It is not easy being a human being. There are so many demands on everyone to succeed in business, relationships and within family. God has plans for you. Perhaps it will come to you in a dream or as an idea. Mine has arrived, and I am thankful I have found my calling to write.

Scribed by Nita Jane

Embrace, relax, meditate and breathe.

Beauty

Beauty is in the eyes of the beholder. What do you see when you perceive great beauty? Is it the land, the sea, the birds of the air, the clouds? The sparkling night sky with all its galaxies and stars? What does beauty mean to you? Is it the new baby? The wonderful creations placed upon the Earth? Whatever it may mean to you is right, for that is your perception.

Guess what? *You* are beauty. *You* are part of the beauty that surrounds you every day. Of course, most humans will look at beauty from the perspective of a runway model. Physical attraction is always depicted as beauty, and there is no denying the people who are indeed blessed with the best genetic makeup found on Earth. But we are all unique within ourselves. You can be beautiful on the outside, but that masks a storm that rages inside.

If you see the true beauty and essence in someone, you possess the same because you are a reflection of what you are looking at. There are many with such a beautiful soul, who are kind in nature, helpful and loving. So, you see, beauty is a word that describes something that is flawless, and it can be physical or spiritual. There is so much beauty in our environment that it is, without a doubt, breathtaking to behold. The landscape, oceans, the cosmic galaxy patterns, art... the list goes on.

Inner beauty is knowing how to love and nurture yourself first. It is not a selfish practice; it is a positive one. For who will look after your wellbeing if you don't? So, please take care of the beauty within so it reflects the external beauty.

Magnificent, that is what you are, in the image of The Creator. Think, and so shall ye be. Born of greatness, ready to take on the rest of your life with precision and gusto, enjoyment and enthusiasm. The world is a better place since you showed up. Embrace your calling, feel the energy arise, go forth and conquer. Try it all, and move on if it does not serve your purpose. Don't waste your time going around in circles, trying to please others. You are here to please yourself. Look after you and never stray from your path. Remember that you are the spark of the Divine, and you can do all things great. Be with people who inspire you and your life, for life is precious, and so are you. Awaken into your happy place and never be afraid. There is so much to do and so little time. You are exactly where you are supposed to be at this time. We love you eternally.

Be at peace with who you are for your beauty resonates through the Universe.

Belonging

Everyone wants to belong somewhere. We yearn for a place in society among our peers, and we strive to fit in. Sometimes, people may mock us, but we still prefer to be in the company of those who ridicule us rather than being alone. It is very sad but true that evolution has placed our DNA system in a collective idealism state. We are born to feel safe in a group environment as we are meant to help and protect each other. However, society is moving towards an individual society, where every person is out for themselves.

Too many within our society die alone. Even those who have a wonderful young life are forgotten as they age; soldiers, pensioners and widowers. We no longer live in villages where everyone knows each other and takes care of each other. We need to be more responsible for one another and look in on those around us, especially those who are vulnerable. A new era has emerged, and with it, more selfish people than ever before. Touch someone else's life if you care to, and make someone's day.

Ultimately all of creation is one.
Division exists only in the mind.

Bible

The *Bible*, they say, is The Creator's word. My question is: Did He really say those words or was it someone else's interpretation of what He may have said? There are a lot of ancient parables written in the *Bible* Stories of biblical times, races of people from an era that is long gone. We have no absolute truth to back up these claims. Messages from the Bible are inspired by God, especially the proverbs I find comforting, such as John 8:12. 'Then spoke Jesus again unto them, saying, 'I am the light of the world'.'

So many verses bring me warmth and security. To even know that He loves me unconditionally is enough to make my heart sing and to know I am never alone and can call on Him, always. Ancient scrolls found are now sitting under the Vatican in Rome. These are the true texts of the *Bible*. It is not called the *Bible*; it is the ancient scribing of God's word, written in Aramaic, the language of Jesus. They were hidden because they hold the secret to a happier and more fruitful life for all mankind.

It was simple: how to end hunger and live collectively; helping each other and learning how to cultivate the land and education on horticulture, agriculture and technology and how to store resources effectively. Harvesting, sustainability and the best practices for maintaining your health. The scrolls share compassion and teach those who are lost in false doctrines the truth about how to live a happier and safer life.

The ancient scrolls hold all the information on the mystery of the pyramids, the crop circles and the presence of extra terrestrials and why they are here and visit frequently. We are visitors to this planet and therefore we need to learn to treat our planet with the respect She deserves.

> *May The Creator bless you and*
> *keep you safe from harm.*

Body

Scribe: The body is such a complex machine that houses all these different components. As human beings, we need to understand ourselves and how it all fits in together.

The ability to scan and see inside the body will be yours for the offering. The ability to see the ailments in another human being's body has been passed down from your ancestry. This will come into alignment when you have balanced your own body and also when you can see the ailments inside of yourself. The ability to read the body is yours for the taking. In time, you will be able to see how the body functions, every artery connecting to tissues, and where the damage is located. You will be able to pinpoint the exact area where treatment needs to take place.

Envision the entirety of all surrounding the patient holistically; look at the lifestyle and the thought patterns and establish what you're looking at to come to a conclusion.

An assessment is obtained first; questions are asked to see a fuller picture of what the cause of the problem within the body may be. From there, you will be able to slow down the disease.

Blue represents the healing power of God. When one is congested with flu symptoms, it is a time of purging to eliminate unwanted debris. The nose represents the ability to smell, taste and breathe. When mucus runs, it signifies the release of old, built-up energy. The throat represents the ability to speak your truth and to change your tune.

How your chest feels indicates pressure; what type of pressure do you feel you are under? What are you worried about?

Higher states of consciousness take practice, action and practice again. The body knows exactly what to do. When the body hurts, the body is in high frequency light. Do not pull into belief systems when the body resonates in a high frequency. Are you listening to the body? Or are you listening to a belief system?

The belief system tells you that the body needs medicines to make it better. The body itself knows how to fix the ailment – we just need to trust. We need to listen to our bodies more. Let go and surrender, and do not try to control a 5D consciousness; the body is light.

Scribe: How does the body speak to us through pain?

Arms – holding on to something that no longer fits your needs.

Back – supports the whole body. Fear of no support system around the inability to rise and be accountable for your own life and actions. Carrying a burden.

Bones – represent the structure collapsing, or foundation crumbling.

Breast – to lose your breast depicts the fear of not feeling nurtured.

Chest – the breast plate covers and protects. If sore, this could mean you are feeling vulnerable.

Ears – what is it that you do not want to hear?

Feet – where are you walking to and how far do you expect to go? To neglect one's feet means you abandon the search for which direction to go.

Fingers – when fingers have been severed and reattached, communication and self-expression has awoken within.

Hands – to grip or hold onto. Why can't you let go?

Legs - afraid of stepping forward. Swelling mean not accepting change.

Neck – supports the head, the most important thing in your body. When the neck is damaged, it can no longer support the head properly. You are seeking greater independence.

Shoulders – provide stability. Why do you think you have no stability?

Skin – if itchy or flaky and irritated, ask: is something or someone getting under your skin?

Toes – stabilise the feet. Balance and support is required.

Consulting medical professionals is essential for accurate diagnosis and treatment.

Scribe: As a receiver of this universal information, here are my personal thoughts on the body:

What can we say about the magnificent piece of complex machinery that is the body other than wow! God made us into a wonderful piece of art, and we are one of his best creations yet, in my opinion. There is so much we still need to learn, and even after thousands of years of evolution, we still haven't got it right. The instructions for a better life are not found on a piece of paper somewhere in your pocket, nor is it found etched in a rock. The instructions lie within each and every one of us. The body will tell you everything if you care to listen. Of course, you feel sensations related to the body, from goosebumps to extreme cold and heat. Then you have the more complicated side of the intelligent body, which is the brain and all the nerve endings firing off at full steam ahead when they are stimulated.

There is also the famous consciousness, unconsciousness and subconsciousness. They are independent of each other. I simply refer to them as the one who is awake, the one who is asleep and the one who stores all information until needed.

This is the only way I understand these very complex 'friends', as I call them. They are a part of every human being. The way we are able to produce offspring still amazes me even though I have four myself and eight grandchildren and am truly blessed. The Creator's miracles are perfection, is all I have to say. There are too many details of what the body can do and how it can heal itself. The list goes on forever. To maintain such a machine, there is such a lot to process and so much stimulation out there in the media with supplements to take, exercise programs, dieting regimes – no wonder we are so puzzled by what we should be doing. We are bombarded constantly from the time we wake in the morning until we are asleep, and we dream and worry whether we've done the right thing.

Each meridian has its own pathway with individual map lines according to their makeup. Internally, we are made up of millions upon trillions of microorganisms that work simultaneously to function as one. When there is interruption in one specific area of the body, there is a hiccup in the system, which causes a jolt – similar to an electrical current – where it runs through the same meridian that the pain is coming from. The electrical current sends waves to try to fix the problem, but when it's blocked, there is a build-up, causing the body to ache in particular places.

To help unblock these areas, first, one must acknowledge the areas affected. Then, picture and feel the blockages with your mind. Send the 'golden' stream of light pulsating through your veins and envision your body as a temple – the holiest of temples you have ever encountered. Be in awe of the magnificence of this temple. Clean your temple with natural products and honour your temple with loving thoughts. Communicate gentle reminders of why you love your sacred temple and why you would not let anything or anybody desecrate your temple. You will defend and nurture your temple until it is returned to Mother Earth, keeper of all.

The more you love what you see, the more you become in tune with Universe and all its miracles abound.

Bravery

The message to mankind is to be loving and humble to each other. Listen to the wind; it calls to us all to take up arms and fight together as a nation to eradicate the beast that devours the host. Give rise to the almighty that will slay the beast with one almighty blow; the serpent will be no more very soon. There will be no more frenzy feeding for this monster, for the love of the Christ Divine will cut it to pieces, never to be seen again. Seek the comfort of each other now and embrace the Divine, and ask to be forgiven, for mercy shall follow. Mankind will not fall but will learn how to manage and sustain each other without the need for greed.

Come out of your homes, human beings, and face the onslaught of the love Divine. He, the almighty king of kings, the server of the universal, Divine Source, understands the awakening process. Know that you are in the centre – the eye of the storm. Ride through it, and do not be afraid, for He is with thee. He will always comfort thee. Celebrate the fact that you all have come through it unscathed.

There is strength in your character, which speaks loudly and clearly of courage and bravery. For you have come through so much in your life and have come out the other end a much wiser and all-knowing human being.

There is always light at the end of the tunnel. Follow the light and awaken.

Breathe

Breathe deep, Dear One. Inhale and exhale. Thank the beautiful trees for their oxygen and shelter, as they are the lungs of the Earth. They also provide their bark for heating and offer their fruit. The trees filter all the pollutants out and give us fresh air to breathe in. Aren't we so fortunate to have such gigantic entities around us? They are alive, just like you and me, and yet we overlook their majestic magnificence. The trees are family; they give us so much, and are never sad when we decide to cut them down for fuel. They serve humanity unselfishly. They also feed us and shelter us from the rain and harsh sun. So, the next time you stand next to a tree, be grateful and thankful that you are still privileged to see and be with one.

Their magnificence is awe-inspiring, and they have witnessed many years of change, and yet they have adapted to the environment in order to survive. A tree is not just a tree; it is a life force. Remember that!

Without breath, we do not exist.

Celestial beings

Scribe: Who are the celestial beings?

Pure, untainted beings. It is difficult for us to fully explain the full version of what and who they are, but we will try and hope it does not confuse you.

They come together as clusters. They cannot function individually. They will cease to exist if they are separated; they have command over the elements. They are all different, and their purpose is to assist those who have been awakened and help them to find their full potential. Some of these beautiful beings are medically trained, hence the fact that they are with you during the Reiki sessions. Some are gardeners helping to nurture the plants, trees, etc. Others are scholars in their fields and have mastered these arts faithfully and have improved on them. All have their specialities; just tap into them and ask. They are here to serve humanity.

Scribe: Where did they come from?

They are from the Source and can be likened to Angels, although it is inaccurate to label them as such.

They, too, are the spark of the Divine; the only difference between you and them is they did not have to evolve on the Earth plain. They were born without human attachments, karma, and everything that makes up a human being.

We can say they are the pure essence of God, for they know nothing else, and emanate all things that love is. They go about their business without interruption and know what they must do to serve humanity. They, too, had a choice to be human, or to be the beings that they prepared themselves to be.

The celestial beings have a stratum of elevation and ranking system, for all must learn and train to elevate themselves. There is an exchange of energy between the human being and the celestial being. The more the human being learns, the brighter the celestial beings become and the more powerful they are to assist the human being. There is a reciprocal agreement on arrival to Earth.

Scribe: Are you saying that we are all born as celestial beings and then choose our own paths?

Yes, Dear One, that is correct in all ways.

Scribe: So, what you are saying is that all life forms above and below are all linked, all one big family?

Yes, to find who you truly are and to have a more fulfilling life with peace and harmony, the human being is required to link. However, many leave the Earth never fulfilling this desire because they don't know what they desire; hence, the lost soul trying to find their place in society, wandering aimlessly without ever knowing their true potential.

Scribe: Is it then safe to say that I have been talking to my higher self and all others in the same realm?

Yes, Dear One, you have merely slipped into the next room or behind the curtain when you wish to meld with us. We have become 'one' with you. We have always been here, but society dictated and encouraged the human being to become more materialistic, ego-driven and greedy. Family groups were becoming a thing of the past; one had to struggle on their own in order to survive instead of living a stress-free life. Pay more attention to Spirit. It will come again, the rising of spirituality in a different form.

My beloved, you are always free to do what you want to do. We do not hover about; we are here whenever you need us. All you need to do is speak, whether out loud or within. We always hear you. We rejoice knowing you found us. We are the higher vibration and will always be protect you. We know that everything you do is done in love, peace and harmony. We will synchronise your body ratio to house the enormity of our energy.

You light up my world in the most wonderful ways.

Change

Old soul, you are beginning to recalibrate and change. You are starting to remember changes within your biological, physical self. Sometimes, you will become dizzy or disorientated. The body is trying to adjust; move with the body and not against it. Where did you spend the most past lifetimes? That is influenced by the kind of diet you're supposed to be consuming in this lifetime. Go into the Akashic Records and see what will work for you. The Earth needs you to change, and the cellular structure will do this. Old habits will start to disappear. Manifest what you need, and it will place you in a situation where there is synchronicity. The lightworker is beginning to become supported by the Universe, and all of humanity will feel the shift. Old energy is changing over the next two generations. There is no timeframe, but all will change for the better.

I never knew that life would change for me as soon as I changed my attitude and thought processes. That's how far I have come since then. So, change is possible if you want to progress in this life.

> *Life is unfolding and changing as we speak;*
> *like the twirling ribbon dances as it changes*
> *its shape held steadfast by the gymnast.*

Channelling

Scribe: Please explain what channelling is?

When one connects with the inner world, the world of knowing and knowledge, there stands before you the ability to ask and unite with one's higher self. It is I, Elohim, here to guide your question.

The dimensions seem confusing; however, they have depth, and there also has to be some sort of order maintained within these realms. We do not allow entities to attach to a human. It is the human that allows such a thing, for nothing is done without permission from the willing party. Create within yourself the Christ light form of love. Know that you are loved, and take that. We are with you whenever channelling is involved.

Many questions are asked of whether there are rituals; the answer is no. There is, however, a dimension of respect around what is happening. Do not take these things too lightly, Dear One, for humans have a way of straying from where they should be focused. We cannot allow you to become too complacent with the whole ordeal.

Become the confident human that you are. Believe in what you are about to accomplish, and do not be sidetracked; stay true and strong, know who you are, and awaken, Dear One, to your calling. Please know that we continually support you and have been told this on many occasions. There is no turning back now. We can only ask you to go forward. Create a perfect place for you to sit and write; we also sit with you. You do not have to think of what to write. Our information shall flow through you.

Be brave, Dear One, let go of what holds you back. We guide you every single day. We are now one. You have connected with us and know this will be a normal existence from now until you leave the Earth. It is not like turning a light switch off or on for we now walk with you. We will guide you to seek medical attention when needed, or we will activate within you the healing frequencies. You may feel that your body vibrates when you're sleeping, this is called fine tuning, almost like a piano being fine-tuned.

Scribe: Thank you for answering all my human questions, Elohim!

My Dear child, we told you before you have been with us before. Only in this existence you are accepting and allowing the light to be free and flow free from you. Once you let go fully, you will not endure human suffering like you do now. We will help you overcome many obstacles.

With Divine deliverance, may the blessings be!

Scribe: *I stand before you, Lord Divine, to thank you all, and the spirit realm, for all that you do for humanity.*

I hear and acknowledge, Dear One. We are of service and are connected.

I am from the light, and I return to the light.

Clarity

Clarity of thought signifies clearer thinking and confirmation of affirming what is correct in our perception. When you clarify things with people, you have a clear indication of what is expected of you, so there is no guessing in the exchange of conversation. It is concise in all matters, and to be clear and accurate saves so much trouble and tension between all parties. So many people can get the wrong end of the conversation, and while it is not always dangerous, it can cause a whole heap of unnecessary confusion and damage. It's easy to clarify what you heard the first time instead of assuming. Clarification is suggested instead of interpreting your own understanding.

At least you will get it right. It is strange how we receive communication but try to make it fit with what we know instead by allowing the receiver to finish their explanation. Food for thought and contemplation.

Follow your purpose and your curiosity will get you there.

Climate change

The gravitational pull of the Earth has become stronger.

Scribe: What does that mean?

More beings are starting to resurface!

Scribe: Why?

To make themselves known to humans.

Scribe: Are they friendly?

They are the star seeds that were planted a long time ago, waiting to awaken once the time was right, which is now. The Earth is going through a transformation, and with it, human beings are beginning to evolve. As coming into a higher awareness, some are not able to cope. Vibrations are getting higher, and so are frequencies.

Control the emotions at this time, Dear One. Do not take things personally, but stand your ground and know your stuff. Being self-assured means you know who you are. Presently, too much emphasis is on climate change. The only way we can truly have climate change is to change the minds of the people behind the industries that are causing the most pollution.

Scribe: How do you do that?

Share your awareness with them; the more people open to Spirit, the more they will realise this environment will disappear without intervention. Although the everyday person is doing their bit to lessen the impact by recycling, etc, it is not enough. Big industries make a big mess. Higher taxes for them will see them change the way they do things. Start to get scientists in to observe and find a cleaner way to work. The information is out there; the government needs to get on board to fund the changes in industries. Tackle the big beasts, and the small ones will also fall.

The further we go into the millennia, human beings cannot stay in the old frequency as the ascension is already upon you, Dear One. The elevation is apparently everywhere one looks of late. You are experiencing many disasters, this is only the beginning for if your leaders do not take global warming seriously, there will be a major downfall.

Scribe: What can we do?

Send energy healing to the Earth, Dear One. Uplift Gaia and help rebuild and repair the gridlines. Some amazing gifts will open for you Dear One, we have readied you.

There is so much heartbreak and devastation at the moment. Dear One, think of the animals, plants and sea creatures that suffer every day at the hands of human beings and their waste, and the impact it has on the land and sea. The disaster that man faces today is a meagre small percentage compared to our animal and plant kingdom. Yes, lives are lost, but very few count the loss of the life forms that hold the planet together. What is happening is nothing compared to what is about to happen.

This is only a test run for all human beings to wake up to their own destruction. The big shift is about to rock all humans off their foundations. When half the planet disappears into the ocean, there will be no warning. The indigenous will feel the shift, and so will the animals. Learn to study their behaviour for when they go to higher ground or start to migrate, things will start to happen.

Evolution has taught human beings to be a lot kinder to the planet, but they continue the carnage of not only themselves but other species that walk the Earth. Look at the weakest part of the planet, then you will know. Where the resources have been mined a lot, and the cavities can no longer be filled, things will start to collapse into it. Sea life is being strangled by debris and will float to the surface. Mother Nature's still in charge; the deep-sea creatures will not be affected, for one day, they too, will walk upon the Earth as predicted and have evolved this way over thousands of years. They are more adaptable than human beings; it is the way of it.

The word evolution does not come close to what it is – it is in fact the 'exchange.' For life, too, becomes worn out and needs a shake-up to develop better strategies to cope with impending danger.

Days are becoming numbered as the Earth goes through a reset. Big and small creatures will start to disappear slowly due to the extent of the polluted atmosphere and waters. Human beings have been given the tools to eradicate all of these manmade disasters but are greedy and will withhold such things in exchange for payment for resources, which they already do.

Scribe: Disasters continue to rage around the world. Why has it been so destructive?

The land is fighting back. For every action, there is always a reaction; Mother Earth will not tolerate it anymore. She will fight back to reclaim what is hers. Unfortunately, in her wake, all things crumble but are later renewed.

We do not know any other species that destroy each other the way human beings do. To wipe out another civilisation for pleasure or for fun is beyond our understanding. We are hopeful that you can all be turned around to see a better life for yourselves. With the help of many light workers that are working right now, it will happen. For to be a light worker, you do not need to be centre stage. Many work tirelessly behind the scenes without recognition. This, my Dear One, is you.

To awaken into a new world is spectacular. A universal shift, with new technology, paradigms and awareness; I am the Universe, I am totality.

Closure

It is a great feeling to bring or see something to the end. Perhaps a project or something that has waited too long and needs to be completed to see the end product. How satisfying to witness such a transformation? To complete a degree and experience such a relief, and to know there is a future after the completion is just wonderful. We may or may not think we are worthy of such a gift, but know that we have worked very hard to get where we are going. So celebrate and reflect on all the times when you wanted to give up.

Strive to do your best in all different situations and circumstances so the hard work and hours, sometimes years, seem worthwhile. Understand that you are more than capable of doing and being anything you want to be. The world awaits your creativity and positive energy. Be brave to take that leap of faith and continue your work to completion.

Sometimes, you may come up against stumbling blocks, but get back into it again and pick up where you left off. The rewards are too great to let things pass you by. Once you have initiated the goal, you must see it through. Try not to abandon your project because you will regret it and beat yourself up. Another thing, try not to tell too many people what your intentions are. Some have their own views on why you can or can't do what you're doing. Let them keep their opinions to themselves; you don't need to listen to negative chatter. Your intuition tells you and guides you every step of the way. All you need to do is have faith and know that what you are doing is right for you. If that doesn't work, try another approach. You can never fail; only learn how to do things better next time. Congratulations to all those who persevere and ride the tide. Your dreams do come true. Kia Kaha – stay strong.

*Take a deep breath – inhale –
exhale, and let it all go.*

Collective

Let us encourage each other and bring out the best in everyone. Like the light that chases the darkness away, we can be that light for someone who may feel a little bit lost. The spark of The Divine is who you are. You have been born to live an earthly existence, and that is to help humanity, for when you help others, you help yourself. We are all interconnected – the trees and beautiful flowers you see outside; everything has energy, and we have become the environment, so we must learn to look after what we have. In doing so, we have a better life. 'Look after each other' is the best advice I have ever heard. It is not until a major disaster occurs that people need each other the most. We should not wait until that happens. Embrace and support everything and everyone around you.

Love costs nothing and is able to penetrate anything everywhere. This is the foundation of all we do. Give and send unconditional love, for love will cure a broken heart or a dreary day and put a smile on someone's face. Never judge, for there is much sadness in the world already, and only love, kindness, compassion and care may lift it.

The Collective are the spiritual beings that sit in the cosmos with the almighty source. They have been created and nurtured to serve mankind; they are the keepers of healing, love and compassion. They have been on the Earth for millions of years, and they include many species of sentient beings. When they are called upon for a particular reason, for instance healing, the beings who are most adept at healing will step forth and assist the human in conducting the healing. There are also others with their specialities in higher forms of engineering, architecture, building materials and macrobiotics – you name it, and the sentient being will be able to assist you. May peace be with you.

> *As mysterious as it may sound, we are all in the same pool of life together; we are not separate. So be nice and gentle to your fellow human beings.*

Communication

Communication comes in various forms: oral, non-verbal, through gesture and telepathy, and writing. There are many other ways to communicate, but these are what you are most familiar with. To express oneself and to understand how you want to bring everything together to make sense, try to focus on an idea and mix it with love, blessings and gratefulness. What is interpreted by the receiver is what they are looking for in the answer.

Why do we communicate? We do this to either get our point across to the other person or to give direction. When you understand fully what you will convey to the other person, life becomes so much easier for the sender and the receiver. Communication involves a two-way radio that needs one person to stop and listen before the other speaks. Human beings have lost the ability to be patient and wait their turn.

All human beings are capable of telepathy. When you sit on a train or bus, and you are thinking about a particular person sitting next to you or ten metres away, they will pick up that transmission in the ether (air). That is why their head turns quickly. They have no idea why, and you are jolted by their response. Perhaps it was a compliment, or maybe it was a judgement; either way, they heard you. That is why it is so important to have loving thoughts for everyone.

"What you say is what you are." This statement still rings true today. We communicate with song and the breeze; frequency is all around us. We just need to stop our busy lives for one minute to hear the crickets, the buzz of the bees and the way they speak to us. They are all in synchronicity with each other, as well as human beings. The silence also communicates; the frequencies are all around – waves are in the air and they come from our electrical devices, which *hum* like bees.

Be nice; be kind; find loving words, not only in your speech but also in your thinking, congratulating people, or when saying hello. The world is a better place when you see someone smile.

I speak from a higher vibration. We talk about energy, airwaves and currents. We are all of that on a wave of discovery. All at once; nothing is separate; that is why human beings struggle with themselves – they cannot separate what is theirs and what is not. That is why one needs to know themselves more and not get caught up in the current 'trend', as we may say. There is, of course, an order to things, places, material, non-material matter, finances, variables, commodities and valuables. All are mere substances to accommodate the human existence. Ask a question – any question – the answer is in the ether or the Akashic Records.

There are many ways to communicate; the deaf do it very well with sign language. Telepathy is another form of sending messages, connecting with the other person through the mind without spoken words. Gesture is another form of communication; it is usually used when two people do not speak the same language but are able to get their intentions across to each other.

Even people who are non-verbal – you will see it in their eyes, especially those who have had a stroke and are unable to move. If you take the time and tune in, you will be able to read them like a book and know exactly what they are looking for and want.

We live in a world where communication is so important. We can talk through psychic mediums with our loved ones who have passed. We all have this ability; it is not exclusive to a few. Spirit communicates with us all the time, but we fail to take the time to listen to our Guardian Angels, celestial beings and ancestors, who are all trying to communicate with us. When we are in prayer, we ask God to help us, bless us and get us through hard times. We tend to forget about Him and go about our business until we are traumatised again. How hard is it to say, "Thank you, Lord, for sending your Angels to help me".

A lot of people say they can communicate with the animals and trees. No doubt they can, for we are all living, breathing entities and are all connected through the universal collective. We were created by the same Source, and yet we are not dissimilar; we are the same. That is why we have the capability to connect with anything living.

> *As the wind blows, the sands shift, so too do the thoughts in the minds of man. May those thoughts be in harmony as they communicate in the language of the Earth.*

Compassion

Compassion is more than doing for others before doing for yourself; it is concern for the suffering or misfortune of people. To practice acts of kindness toward another is compassion, to say encouraging words to another when you can see their suffering, and to go beyond your own caring. Confused? Well, to put it simply, you become in tune with the needs of others and what they are experiencing or feeling. Life for you becomes more bearable because you know you have offered your support to someone else who may be suffering, whether it be mentally, physically or otherwise.

Some people want to know if there is someone out there who can help them. There are great leaders among us who have offered their services because they have witnessed families going without food or shelter. Very few possess the capacity for these acts of kindness. Some have been through their own life crisis and experiences and are aware of the suffering they have already endured, therefore they want to help others going through the same thing.

Compassion is unconditional love; a selfless act towards self and others. How can you treat yourself less and others with such conviction and compassion? We are, without a doubt, a species that thrives on being loved and showing love, yet we rarely show it to ourselves. The Creator has sent his beautiful, precious heavenly beings, the humans who were given extra chromosomes at birth so they can teach humanity how to love, laugh, smile and never judge. They are The Creator's blessings to humanity and have pure compassion.

> *Life is full of unconditional love; we just need to know where to look.*

Complete

What makes you feel whole and complete? Perhaps it is the end of a cycle for you where there is a mission that you fulfilled. I'm sure that would make you feel whole, especially if there was struggle involved. We human beings create too much drama for ourselves, yet expect to live in harmony. Well that's a joke! You are complete the way you are; we must encourage this mindset in everyone around us.

Our expectations of ourselves are too high; we need to learn to take it easy and not to criticise. We always think we're not good enough, not clever enough. But I am here to tell you that you are this and more. We all have our own way of dealing with the feelings and insecurities we have developed. Simply ask for help if you need to, there is no shame in asking. What you're doing is getting someone to reflect on something you already know.

Acknowledge that and move forward from your current dilemma. You will feel better, that's for sure. You were whole and complete when you arrived on the Earth as a newborn. The circumstances you were born to shaped the person you are today – all influenced by your surrounding culture, the colour of your skin, the country you were raised. Environmentally and physically, you were stimulated to act in a certain way. As you mature, you either keep what you've learned or decide for yourself what you want to keep and what you want to create for yourself and your family. If there is a pattern that you want to change in your life, then please do so. Otherwise, that will filter through to your next generation of children. Of course, keep all the meaningful ones. We all have a place in society but continue to berate ourselves. The Universe sings our praises and loves us unconditionally.

> *Like the links in a chain, we keep climbing to reach our destination. One link at a time we will get there; I have confidence in you.*

Compliment

To be paid a compliment uplifts the soul. It means you have done something extraordinary. Even though you may not have seen it yourself, others have noticed. If you are one of these people who go about their business and do not go around looking for praise, then you are very humble indeed. The unseen, helpful warriors always looking out for others before themselves; they call them the unsung heroes, the ones who do not seek fame. When the war broke out, it was known that many soldiers had become superheroes and saved many lives. Their unselfish deeds did not go unnoticed, and some received the Purple Heart for bravery.

When someone pays you a compliment, say thank you because you are indeed deserving of such praise.

> *Your smile is contagious, all those around you will catch it, so smile often.*

Confidence

Scribe: The sun is shining and the earth around me is stable. I am feeling a lot more confident about everything in my life at this point in time, may it continue to be so. I am here to embrace the world in all that I am; to fulfil the life I was sent here for; to believe that I am bigger and better than what I ever thought.

Dear One, you have come a long way in your journey to find who and what you are. You have now accepted every single part of yourself. Accept the rewards that are now bestowed upon you.

We love you eternally. Your work is just beginning beautifully and effortlessly. Time to focus, time to let go, time to be prosperous in everything you do. Speak to the Angels. Know they guide you every single day. The touch of your hand, the hug, the kiss – all comes from us.

Wherever you touch someone, walk and talk, they feel our presence – the presence of the Divine. Walk forth, stay humble, be at peace always. No need to be emotional, for we will stand by you to give you the words and confidence to speak.

Know that in time the pictures will become clearer as you progress, and everything will flow as it should; there will be no struggle, no financial pressure anymore, for we have timed everything to the last minute. Synchronicity is the key; when and where are the questions. God's timing is precise. Everything runs in alignment with other events happening at that time. The bigger picture means the past, present and future are coming together as one, with alignment.

Only you can make a difference in where you want to be. Acceptance is the key!

Connection

We are of pure golden light and we come from many destinations and cover so many galaxies. Our vision is your vision and that is to see all human beings synchronise with one another and to go back to caring for the planet. Know that you are all part of nature. The awakened peoples all over the world knew this, and still do.

Be at peace with yourself; we love you eternally. Beneath the façade is the awakening. As humans, you're likely to parade around those who reflect how you are feeling at the time once you start to transition to a better state of mind where everything becomes clearer.

Mind, body and soul – the awareness arrives and takes over your perception of everything around you. Your worldview takes on a different persona. Light arrives at full force, thunder echoes in the skies and the sound of rain becomes louder as you begin to tune into the new frequencies and the new way of doing. No longer are there emotional ties that try to separate you from yourself. Holding grudges will no longer work. It is time to go back to your ancestors to take your rightful place as an elder alongside your relatives.

Going back means going forward in your journey of life. Remember the way your ancestors lived; how to hold your Mana (Divine power) or spiritual energy and the universal life force. Always remember that the ancestors hold your hand, every step of the way, slowly giving way to the roots of who and what you are bought here for. Reclaim what is yours and take ownership for your family and those that will follow in your footsteps.

We will guide your willingness to go back to the land, the land of your forefathers, the land of your birth.

> *The work is inside of you; that*
> *work must be done!*

Creativity

Creativity is not just about the arts and writing; it is much more. We all have special talents; we just need to find them. For instance, someone very creative recycled the book and papers that I am scribing these words upon. We humans can do anything given a chance and someone who believes in us. We only need faith to bring us through the rough times. You have a brilliant mind, and there are wonderful possibilities. You are my love, the true existence of life itself. Find your truth and talents, and you will leave the Earth much happier. In love we are; be at peace, Dear One.

From the master carver to the gardeners who cultivate the earth to help things grow, inside us, we all have the ability to create something from nothing, from cooking delicious food to painting and sculpting famous works of art. What would you like to create for yourself? Perhaps it is a boat or vehicle you would like to restore? No matter what it is, get those ideas and creativity happening. The world is waiting for you to create something incredible. A new invention, perhaps?

Unleashing your creativity is the start of a new chapter for yourself. How would you like it to begin? God talks about creation and when He created the Earth and skies. Ideas and dreams all manifest into creativity. It is wonderful to watch someone create something from a block of wood or material spun into a garment. Wool turns into a jersey, mittens and socks. Houses are built by very skilled people. The implements we write with are all creations. What is yours?

Creative minds bring about creative attributes.

Crop circles

Let us begin with time. A long time ago, seeds were planted. What kind of seeds, you may ask? Seeds that bury themselves deep within the Earth, so deep they enter Earth's core system. The fruit that emerges from these seeds is called the Earth Centaurs, the keepers of the grid, the Guardians of planet Earth.

Every so often, they are called upon in order to find and track signals that are sent as vibrations under Earth's crust. The Centaurs locate the signals and send directions to where the crop circles are to appear. The crop circles are directions to the gateway or pathway, which galactic beings must travel. Once travelled and followed correctly, the beings reunite the Earth with gravity. Otherwise humans will float uncontrollably above the Earth's surface. You could say that these beings are made of magnetic bodies. These entities have been created for one purpose only, and that is to keep balance on the Earth using their magnetic pull.

The crop circles signal to them to surface in a particular area that needs healing. Scientists have not let humans know this and keep them guessing. Of course, Stonehenge is also one of these gateways – all is to help the Earth to function as best it can. Sadly, it is only running at 65 to 76 per cent. We have earthlings that also work with the grid of the planet, each doing their bit to stabilise the core centre so that no more damage is done. Crop circles appear in different circumferences and sizes, depending on the damage that's been done to the Earth's core. Only the magnetic beings are able to communicate with the crop circles, for it is Mother Earth who leaves the inscription and design to show the damage caused. You could say it is a map of where to repair and find the problem – a calling card.

Humans think the crop circles were developed above ground, not so! As above, so below.

> *When receiving the right messages,*
> *we are transformed.*

Crystals

Have you noticed that the colours of crystals are changing? Purple, blue, orange, green, violet, turquoise, amber, white, combination of all. Different vibrations for different colours. Different sound frequencies for different colours.

The practitioner places the stones along the meridian and the stone vibrates to the specific frequency of the body temple. Some stones are not compatible with some patients; therefore it will be of no use to try and align the chakras perfectly in order to heal the body of its ailments. Kinesiology will help to recognise the correct stone. One size does not fit all. We are the same, however, our soul developments differ in all of us. Use the correct tools if you want to be a chakra balancer.

Human beings are evolving, and so is their body makeup. Now more than ever before, young ones are coming through with totally different DNA systems, so drop the old way of healing – it is of no use now. No rituals are required. Guidance is needed more for the young ones because, although they are advanced, they have no idea what they are dealing with. Hence, many chose to leave and go home rather than ride the waves of life.

We are all connected, and as the crystals activate through high frequencies throughout the Earth, those crystals that are on the surface will vibrate to different sound waves. The way we use crystals will also change. The vibrations are stronger now and the crystals beneath the Earth begin to *hum* to a lower-toned frequency within the Earth's gravitational pull.

The colours are changing to match the human frequencies. The magnetic pull of the Earth is also causing clear gases to be released from underground. Scientists can go there now and test the air. The gases are replacing human beings' abilities to breathe, hence the outbreak of the so-called influenza. It's all got to do with the shift; if there is no shift, there is no elevation. Gamma waves are causing a lot of disturbances for human beings; they are disrupting sleep patterns, causing chaos for human beings' ability to function fully.

Other disturbances are a factor; they are omnipresent. The Creator wants us to learn how to be civil to each other and to stop the bullying, hateful crimes. If you remain in that space, be prepared to go home, for The Creator will no longer tolerate that volatile sense of disrespect.

Know that I am here, and as any parent knows, there are consequences for those who do not adhere to the warnings. You will not return until you have learned not to do these things. As we said before all have choices. The strongest can be struck down with sickness, never to recover.

> *I am all. There is no other like me. I do not come from ego. I am the Father/Mother.*

Cycles

Scribe: What can we do to help mankind to uplift ourselves during this crisis situation?

There is a time when all will be revealed. There is no need to worry or pretend nothing has happened, for this is a big deal. Globally, communication will shut down on a big scale after the virus has run its course. You see, Dear One, the virus not only attacks the human system but will attack external influences as well.

Life as we know it will be forever changed to fulfil the evolutionary cycle of mankind. Be brave to step forward and embrace each wonderful day as it comes into existence, for new days bring new ways and waves of comfort. Greet the day as though it were your last, for that day will not come again. Be kind, be thoughtful and humble; protect your wonderful life; it's all you have here on this Earth. Be grateful and thankful for all kinds of wonderful things in your life, more importantly your family and friends, the ones who protect you, love you, teach you, and are always there for you, no matter what.

We are now in Revelations: the end of the *Bible*, but not the end of humanity. Life will go on, as it always has done, for millions of years to come. We will come back in different external bodies and start again. Seek the same Source, ask the same questions and believe we have been enlightened. The idea is to awaken a lot earlier in life so as not to waste your time on Earth searching for the same things. Learn all there is to learn. Embrace all there is to embrace. Feel the beautiful Earth that surrounds you. Love and feel the sun on your face, the smell of freshly cut grass, the fragrance of flowers and the rolling sea. Know that you are indeed alive, and you are part of the evolution of mankind.

You have all forgotten how to feel nature running through your veins like water, and the smell of the crystal clean air, the ripple of the water as it leaves sustenance for foliage as it winds itself down through the valley, leaving behind newly touched grooves in the embankment. Butterflies and birds are everywhere; the dragonflies flit in and out, teasing each other. There are insects galore, the gardeners of the earth. You are also part of this great magical existence, with euphoric beauty and mesmerising sunrise and sunset. We know the virus has hit human beings, mankind, swiftly and affected many lives. Turn to nature for the answer, for it is within the plants. Green healthy plants that hold the sun will kill the virus. Eat plenty of green leafy produce to avoid the plague. Food is plentiful; choose the right foods.

Scribe: At this moment everything seems surreal, as though we are living in another world and witnessing something through a window frame.

The epidemic has become a reality for all to accept at this time and to go with it. You cannot fight it, nor can you despise or hate the darkness that invited itself. Accept that this is the way it is for now, and things will change sooner rather than later. My question for you, Dear One, is what changes have you made within yourself since this virus was first detected? How has it changed you as a person? What is it that you would like to change about yourself while you are soul searching? Let's be honest, hopefully being kinder to yourself and to others around you. This is not a time to hold grudges or create misery for yourself.

This is a time of extreme healing and forgiveness to take place. Learning to live with yourself, love and be one with self. For being in love with self means, of course, you are in love with the Divine Herself. There is no other love more powerful, more loving and more compassionate than that of the pure essence of God Almighty. Emerge from all of this a happier, healthier individual ready to give healthy healing to those in need.

Every day seems a struggle, every second, every minute and every hour. Ask, and we shall guide you. The music and the sound of peace are about listening with your soul and knowing that I am here. Be gracious and deliver unto us the cure for all in this state of panic. Forgive those who have done wrong, and Lord, we kneel in front of your feet to let you know you are king of kings and lord of lords, and we hear you and acknowledge what needs to be done.

This too will pass. Life as you know it will change for the better. New, innovative ways of thinking will give rise to the old paradigms and linear ways of thinking. Dear One, embrace the new and let the old fade away. Develop within yourself and give birth to new ideas, new ways of living and doing things. Hold fast to great challenges and do not be afraid to step into the arena and accept the challenge.

You have all been delivered another chance of living the way you want and how you want. The trees are the key to filtering the virus, for they are as ancient as Earth herself. Listen as they weep with humanity, a heavy sigh. The mighty oaks filter the carbon dioxide that is riddled with the virus and know that the air you now breathe depends on how much fuel you feed the trees and plants. Dear One, there are natural filters that give the human being the purest air possible.

As one month ends and another begins, you have all reached the pinnacle of your reality, the ability to see what is real and what is not. The future holds nothing of significance at this stage, Dear One, for the future is the beginning of the now. Do something that makes your soul sing, a reminder of all things great in your life. For gratitude is one of the healthiest ways to project how you feel about your situation. Whether great or small, it is acknowledgement of what the Universe provides for us every single day.

Be kind to each other and know your truth and do not be tempted by anyone else's greed for external wealth. Know who you are and what you want, do not allow others to dictate to you and be clear and precise in all manner of being. You are the master of your own life and reality; do not let others change that. Learn how to negotiate and not to give a full answer for anything straight away. We send healing out to all of humanity at this time.

Scribe: As I gaze out across the scenery, I envision myself skimming across the water as quick as possible. I am virtually flying, and the wind is in my hair with the clear water below. The experience is most gratifying.

What has been said before will forever be, for history indeed repeats itself.

Death and rebirth

Scribe: What happens when we 'slip off into the next room', as we call it?

There is nothing to fear, my Dear One, for you all must return home at some stage. The main requirement is here on Earth. Make time to create for yourself a truly spectacular life. A life that resonates and fits with where you want to be. Every human on this planet searches for us at some stage in their lives.

Scribe: Why, as humans, can we not be given that piece of the puzzle when we arrive rather than spending half our lives running around in circles looking for that which is our higher selves?

Dear One, you humans are all at different stages of your development or evolutionary cycles; some humans have come to Earth already knowing but then become conditioned by life's circumstance. You have freedom of choice while you are here. Explore and enjoy your stay while you can because miracles happen every day. We rejoice in knowing you have found the Source and the potential you have. Run with it.

> *Only through darkness can we*
> *see the stars above us.*

Dear traveller

When decisions are made, we must carry them through. Stick to the plan and try not to digress from where you are supposed to be. Be a role model for the coming generations and ensure that there is a concrete foundation for them to follow. Follow your dreams and aspirations, and know that God has you in His sight. You are His first true love and nothing you do is wrong.

We all have lessons we have reincarnated to learn. So, learn well and gather the knowledge that you need to progress in this life. Everything is in your hands, and only you know what's best for you and your walk. Stay grounded and positive. Let the light illuminate your path, for the journey might be long, but when you take the right path, it is a joy to behold. Love, be kind, stay humble and be compassionate to those you know and those you are yet to know. May God be with you on your travels. We love you eternally.

Your life is in your hands; what you do with it will be exciting.

Dedication

It takes dedication to do what you do. Focus is something we strive for, discipline and repetitive patterns help us to stay where we are in the now. So, find a practice that will help you to focus and stay stoic in whatever it is. Do not show your vulnerability, but do show your strength and power. Your life will be made easier if you know what you're doing and where you are going. Find your purpose and remain dedicated to expanding your knowledge on the subject; it is no use sitting there doing nothing. Share your newfound knowledge with others. You never know when you may need their help as well.

They are the ones who think the same way you do; their idealism mirrors your own. Therefore, that is your family while you are on Earth. However, some may resonate with other souls as well. Your biological family are those who understand you better and are able to help you on your journey of discovery, for they are the hardest to get along with and can test your patience. It is exciting to find your cluster family as well to fulfil your destiny and to finally bring closure to your search. I am honoured to work with such amazing and great people. They have come into my life at exactly the right time, for I could not have done this myself. I am very grateful to the Universe and all the sentient beings that surround me every day. They keep me balanced and protect me and my family and friends always.

> *Fill the pages of your being with all that you ever dreamed and desired, the visions you created, and the journeys yet to be travelled. Experience it all and expect the unexpected. Engage with everything that surrounds you. Enjoy the challenge.*

Depression

This section deals with depression and suicide. Please visit the Resources section at the back of this book if you need professional support.

When I hear of so many young ones taking their lives so early, it hurts my heart. It must be difficult to live with the darkness that engulfs them, which seems so severe. Their loved ones are left in the dark to figure out what happened. The loved ones left behind seek therapy to overcome their grief. Therapy is good for some, but we will never understand what is really going on inside a person. The turmoil and the relentless torture that one must experience inside must be traumatising and agonising for the person, with nowhere for the torment to leave, as much as others try to make it go away.

Perhaps the individual may need some kind of spiritual awakening or awareness to see how they can work through the spirit side of who they really are. Some are sceptical and afraid of the unknown. Still, when we uncoil our past lifetimes, we see patterns that may correlate with what we are currently experiencing. We need to start talking more about these things that bother us and help those who struggle with life in general. The more conventional way of addressing these issues is, of course, seeking out counsellors and psychologists, who both do a fantastic job.

The most fundamental things in one's life are knowing who you are and realising you are loved, not only by your family and friends but by the Source, or whatever you may call God. The One who bought you here to Earth in the first place. You do not realise the impact you may have on other people's lives while you are upon the Earth.

By taking your life, you are taking away the opportunity for those around you to spend time with your wonderful energy. Everywhere you go, you must leave a mark on someone. Whether it is something you may have done for that person or something you may have said. Encouragement and love is all one wants at the end of the day. Speak with compassion for each other. Be at peace, my love.

Believe in love. Believe there is a higher energy and source out there that takes care of us. One day, you will join that Source with the rest of your family and ancestors who have passed on. When you go, you will leave a legacy of memories behind so the next generation will not forget who you were.

Forgive all those who have hurt you because they never knew better. Disconnect yourself from the past and the future because what really counts is what is going on right now in your life. Make it bigger and better. Shine your light brighter; that is my advice for you today and always.

What a waste of time, floundering in the dark. I am sure those who had no choice but to leave the Earth because of their illness would gladly trade places with those who find life difficult and don't want to be here. There is no judgement, and there are circumstances as to why people want to leave. But I will not get into that debate. A lot of souls have not completed their journey and yet exited prematurely. Their whole lives were ahead of them, and some even left behind young families. I find that extremely sad.

When the Father calls you home, whether you are ready or not, you too will leave without a warning. We all have an expiration date, and we do not know when it will be. So place your mark or stamp in a society that will remember you, especially your family. How many generations will come and go before you collect dust on your photo and become one of the ancestors that your great-grandchildren may not really know? Leave them a legacy of hope, love, and above all, show the true meaning of life and how to live it.

See, we are all made up of the same substance. We are all connected like the roots of a tree. What you need to realise is that some of the emotions that you experience may not belong to you, so instead of reacting to them and starting to panic, you must learn to distinguish what is our own and what is not. Take the time to feel the sensations; know that it will pass. The second we react to an emotion that does not belong to us, we own it.

Scribe: How can we determine what's ours and what is not?

Get to know your own character; know that you do not react to such nonsense and will not allow anything to cloud your own judgement about who and what you are.

Scribe: How can we reach out, and how can we support those who want to take their own life?

Be kind. Loving. Let them know that you have no judgement, and above all, let them speak and sit in silence. While in silence, ask the Lord our God to send His glorious light so that they may see Him and know they are loved. You cannot change what is, but you can change the way you see things in your own light. Even if you cannot change what is, you can be a light for others to guide the way.

> *Never be afraid. The light will chase the dark away.*

Destiny

Remember you are the creator of your own destiny. Lessons and experiences are all we are here to do. Earth is the densest planet in the Universe. Earth's school is very difficult because you cannot get out of it until you have finished drawing the same circumstances to yourself over and over again and have finally learnt the lesson. This will happen even if it is something you would not care to repeat.

We keep making the same mistakes over and over again; this is the wheel of karma. If you don't get it right the first time, you will return to Earth to complete the lesson. Same circumstances, same types of people, but you will all inhabit different bodies. So, learn all you can while you are here; understand why you do what you do. Know it is all created by you – most people do not want to hear that. They go around blaming everyone else; don't let that be you! Wake up, beautiful spirit. Awaken and live the best life you can.

> *It is not what you are, it is what you've decided you want to be. It takes courage to look for the passion to do something that you love doing.*

Direction

Everything starts from inside and is manifested out. Spiritual leaders can give insight into the elevation of one's soul and spirit. What do you believe in spiritually?

To know oneself is to know spirituality, to know that you are part of the Divine; that love that flows forth with every breath you take. You were born of pure heart and not tainted; your experiences on Earth have determined what you are and where you're going in this lifetime. Take heed, Dear One, for I have spoken. Listen to the deep roar of the sea and wonder at the beauty of the trees in the forest. Hear the water as it slowly trickles over the rocks, which lead down through the valley.

Listen to the birds chirping and the wind blowing the leaves around as they rustle in the breeze, catching your windblown hair. Embellish the wonders of the world around you; look beyond what you see and imagine a world like no other. This is where you sit, Dear One, never alone, always loved and forever pure, never contaminated. In absolute bliss radiance and abundance, teeming with life. This is where you reside, in this happy place, the place of Gods, Angels and Grand Masters. Here, they will answer all your questions; here, you may sit with them. Here, you can relay the messages we send. Find peace with yourself; these are not just words I give you; these are to be followed, to be understood and to be listened to.

Great work to be had and wonderful messages to keep in mind. Facts to follow, and truth to be told. Actions to be taken, and light beings to show yourself and share.

We, as The Collective, have full faith in your delivery. To deliver to those who seek the information. Grand is the voice of love and truth. Perseverance, patience and allowing oneself to be completely engulfed in the divine energy of pure love. Shine that God light for all to see and share his wonderful love and healing with whoever walks into the space; know that you are surrounded with love and protection, always. Know that we walk with you; we talk with you. We protect you from anything that may cause harm.

Everything we touch and feel is all energy, even the things we think and do.

What is your intention when you help someone? What have you got to gain? Is it that the decision you made was for them? Did you do it without thinking? Regardless, the universal law dictates what and where these intentions are. You may think that you are in control. However, there is a process of synchronicity around the 'right place at the right time', all of this is precisely executed in time and space. We only have a portion of what is to come. The rest is through the contract you signed before coming to Earth and the experience you expected.

Seek and ye shall find all that you are looking for. Stop. Focus and ask yourself where might you find what you are looking for and how might you attain such a prized possession? Ask and you will be given what you have asked for. Be precise in what it is that you have ask for; every minute detail is recorded and given exactly the way you asked. Be wise in your asking.

The time has come for all human beings to awaken and realise their body houses the most magnificent machine in all of the cosmos. Learn how to drive such a machine and know that when you have reached the right capacity, all things open out, and your life upon the Earth is made so much easier. Life becomes a breeze when you stay on track. Everything will come to you easily. There will be no sickness, no drama in your life and all becomes serene. To get to the state of bliss, one must let go of all that holds you in the material world. Human beings become tied up in their material possessions, and this stops progression and spiritual growth because the focus is there, not here.

We understand the need to feed, clothe and put a roof over the heads of your children and family. However, you don't need to overdo it with material goods that keep piling up. When you pass, those material goods will remain and probably be given to others. So, try not to accumulate too many unwanted possessions; they are only temporary fixtures in one's life. Celebrate in learning spiritual practices and guidance to harness the greatest gift that God has given to man – the understanding of who you truly are.

In order to do this, there has to be an alignment that shifts to ensure your life becomes exactly the way you wanted it. Sometimes, you will experience things in your life that are not nice at all. It is all part of growing and understanding while moving forward and improving your soul's existence. We do our best to balance the human being who has chosen a horrific existence. But it is all part of learning. The worst thing that can happen is you finally find yourself home again, awaiting a new life in a new existence. Experience life on Earth; it is truly one of God's miracles. Take in as much as possible, absorb and listen! Enjoy, Dear One.

May the light shine to point the way.

Disasters

Scribe: I see a swirl very much like a tornado; what is it I am seeing? The tornado is dark.

It is not for you, it is a negative cause or charge. Although a tornado sweeps everything clear and leaves devastation, those that are affected are bought together for a reason. At the time all seems lost, but friendships are made along the way and humans become more loving and understanding because they have one thing in common – they have lost everything.

Death and devastation equals love and understanding. Coming together as a community, rather than as those who have more than others. It's about helping people who are less fortunate than yourself. Commonality breathes life into all, knowing that you are part of and not excluded or separate.

My Dear, leap forward and do not flounder anymore and wallow away. Stand tall without arrogance and ego like the mighty Totara tree. Your ancestors stood like this, their abilities you have inherited. They were strong, mighty beings; they served The Creator well. You will now have your own path to pave, for life has evolved. You are of their essence and hold similar values, and now you must improve on them through to your next generation. They, too, will surpass where you will leave off.

Beauty lies all around you, people, place, the world in its entirety. Look for the good in all, great or small; beauty also extends beyond the physical being.

Scribe: What would you say to humanity directly?

We would say, please love one another as you do yourself and family and friends. But some people don't like themselves or their family. In this case, there is a choice.

Prepare for destiny; to us, it means merriment, love and honesty, for that is what occurs when all manner of Earth's movements, such as hurricanes, blizzards, earthquakes and many more disasters happen. Ask yourself why? The aftermath will bring human beings together in the thousands – in some cases, millions. If not, we will not be able to witness how loving and caring human beings can be towards each other. The lives human beings lead are indeed solitary. The only way we can get humanity together is to show them how to come together in unison. Therefore, we send tsunamis and earthquakes to awaken you all. This is termed by many as God's wrath, but God does not have anger toward his children.

The Earth shifts at a timely rate, human beings know they are not supposed to build houses, factories, railways, highways etc in certain places but continue to do so. When storms are present, human beings have experienced a brief encounter with loved ones that have passed while being swept up in a storm's fury.

Have you ever been part of a disaster only to find that human beings have come to assist where otherwise, they would not have? So, to us, doom has a different meaning and vibration; it is not all gloomy. I can understand that some people are killed, which is heartbreaking indeed. However, they have chosen to exit with multiple other souls. It is okay; do not be alarmed. Where there is grief and loss, there's also rebirth, renewal and love for mankind.

The distance between man and the Father is closer than one thinks. I don't know why people keep looking towards Heaven when The Creator is everywhere. We are the source. We come from the source. Start to remember the source of all, big and small, and live in this world the best you can. Rewrite your own destiny; you do not have to stick to what has been foretold for you. Rise up. Do your best. Be your best; love, be kind, be grateful.

Remember, to awaken, you need to clear the rubbish that impedes your growth. Know me more, and I will guide you, love me more, and I will show you who you truly are. Remember who you are, Dear One, you are the beloved child of the Universe, The Creator of all.

> *"Weeds are flowers, too, once
> you get to know them."*
> – A.A. Milne

Disease

If you perceive to have a disease and it isn't genetic, you are actually creating it. You are within yourself a community of millions of cells, and every cell is intelligent. They respond to your central voice, which is the mind. The function of the brain is to perceive the signals, interpret these signals, then send the information to the cells to guide their behaviour. This creates your reality.

The placebo effect is something that will help you even if it is a sugar pill that you believe is the real medicine; studies show it can heal a disease. It wasn't the pill that healed you, it was the thought of the pill being able to heal the disease. Negative thinking may harm you. If you believe something is good for you, it will be good for you. Likewise, if you believe something is harmful for you, it will be bad. Stress hormones will shut the immune system down or slow it. Everyone has diseases; it is the immune system that needs to remain healthy in order to protect the body.

Scribe: What about the babies that are born with chronic illness?

Dear One, just look upon their Angelic faces. They have come of their own accord, and they know they have come to experience love through family and all the dynamics that go with losing a child. They are briefly here on Earth to help the extended family love each other unconditionally and come together to support each other through the loss. Dear One, losing a loved one, especially a baby or child, is very traumatic. How one reacts and for how long, nobody can tell. We only know that you must not forget to live, for that is what you are here for.

Remember, your loved one will be safe with us. They can never be hurt again. The only thing that hurts us is to watch you waste your time on Earth yearning for those who have left to go home. We cannot send them back into the same vessel they left in; it is worn out like clothing. Please let your loved ones rest and know that you will be reunited one day. You, too, will go home, so make the most of the time you have here. Love, give love and live like you have never lived before. We delight at your graduation of elevation.

The essence of life is love.

Dream

Why do you think we dream? Some dreams are bizarre, and others realistic and can also be frightening. Wherever they come from, dreams can bring inspirational ideas or warning signs. We live our lives the best we can within this lifetime and have an accumulation of many lifetimes past. What dreams you have can affect you mentally and physically, especially when you feel that the dreams appear to be real, and you may want to act on them because you cannot distinguish between reality and false projections. It can be quite confusing to remember what the dreams mean and try to put the puzzle pieces together. Are they telling you something?

Dreams are to remind us of what a wonderful instrument we are. We receive so much information and clarification in our dream state. We can also receive premonition. So please do not dismiss anything you may feel is not right. Usually, your instincts will tell you exactly what you need to know. Inspiration is also given in your dream state, although not everyone remembers their dreams. They can also bring nightmares and terror to the most vulnerable people. Dreams can come from past life remembrances that have been etched in the soul somewhere.

Perhaps there is a trigger for some people that send nightmares to them? There seems to always be a reason for dreams. Especially if you remember them fully, maybe there is a warning. Interpret your own dream. After all, it has come from your own subconscious.

*Awaken from your slumber and
put your dreams into action.*

Empathy

I am here, my love, my child of the Universe! Here to embrace you as a mother does to a child. For too long, you carry the hurt of the world. Release all your woes; let me take them from you and become whole. Do not drag with you the state of others, for they are not yours to carry. With empathy and compassion, you can overcome any hurdles placed in front of you. Experience the real love you have been searching for. We reside in you and with you. Love and be loved; enjoy life; that is why you are here. Experience the highs and lows, the good with the bad. Learn to control your emotions, mainly fear. Burden is not something one should carry. Life would become very complicated if it were so. Especially if it is someone else's burden, drop it and never pick it up again.

Look at your life, Dear One; explain to me and write a list of what you feel is holding you back. Are there any barriers? You are not like others! You have your own unique style and energy. Energy comes from within, and the energy must be dispersed outward to be shared in love and with love.

*Random acts of kindness, may
they follow you everywhere!*

Emotions

The wind-up before the emotion is unbelievable. When you have a big wind-up, all it takes is something small to spark the emotion, and before you know it, it has escalated into something uncontrollable. Thoughts start to fly around, and so do assumptions. It is very hard to control, so how does one control their dilemma?

Don't let it get to the point where you are about to explode. We create drama for no reason when we do not know all the facts. When something arises like that, be sure you know the full story instead of guessing because guessing gets people into trouble, especially when the incident is not as bad as first thought. Emotion can really mess with your head; before long, it can become incredibly huge and out of control. Don't let it live in your space because your space is perfect, and there is no room for that rubbish. Stay strong!

*Find the spark that once was.
When you find it, keep it alive!*

Empowerment

People want to be empowered, stand on their own, and face any kind of situation. While we are on a quest to empower ourselves, we can empower others through positive feedback in all they do. Encourage those around you and remind them they are doing an amazing job. Listen to people and their needs if you can.

Affirmations are a great way to keep positive stimulation in your mind. They reaffirm the way we feel about ourselves, they help us to focus on what is more important in life rather than thinking about superficial rubbish.

All I can say is love yourself with all there is, and remember that there is only one path to follow. Although the journey may seem long and obstacles may be in your way, I am confident you will overcome them all. Engage with like-minded individuals who have your best interests at heart. There is no need to try to fit into a group of people who do not fit with you. We are here for a short amount of time; make the most of it.

The gift of life is eternal.

Energy

There is energy all around us; we can't see it, but we can sure feel it. It comes in waves. An aura is energy, and some people can see them as colours. These colours are read by healers in the health profession who can interpret where the area in the patient's body is ailing. This is called alternative practice and may benefit those who seek this type of treatment, which seems to be non-invasive compared to conventional medications, as stated by those who have had both.

Emotions can be detected through energy. As a collective, many people are gathered in one spot with the same intent and consciousness and are able to heal and uplift those who are not well physically and mentally. It feels like electricity surging through the body. Energy from one person is great, but more than one and it has the potential to become a miracle to cure those who need healing.

The planet has masses of energy within the crystalline gridlines, and the magnetic pull on the Earth, as well as gravity, are other energy sources. The new energy gives way to the old. Old paradigms are shifting, and New Age books are flooding the market and bookstores. The internet is introducing a lot more practitioners to people, uplifting the vibration globally.

Stand your ground and never let anyone take advantage of your beautiful energy.

Energy healing

See the colours change within the body; watch the shift from dark through to light. Pinpoint the dark shades in the body and watch the correct colour surge through. So, is your ability now, Dear One, to see the entity in this way. Connect with us, and we will guide your hands and our energy to uplift and assist. Remember, we only activate the patient's energy; we do not interfere with anything else. It is a human myth to think there is an exchange of energies, or karmatically, you will take someone else's energy from them. It is not possible to do this; all that thinking is scaremongering and does not serve you. Rejoice in the fact that nothing can hurt you, for we are with you always, protecting and loving you.

My beloved, the energy is distributed among those entities that work with you, thus the light-heartedness of it all. A healer should never feel tired or drained or heavy or anything like that. Healers are to feel light, alive and fully focused, and not be in la la land. They should actually feel energised themselves. For Spirit will take all of it with love and with great respect. The healer steps aside and allows the spirit healers to allow the flow of energy channelled to the right areas. The source comes through to assist.

You are the beacon, the one human beings will trust. We are the unseen healers who stand with you throughout the whole process. Without you, there will be no trust in us to work with these souls that need assistance in healing. For the human being would have sought a healer or asked to be healed in one way or another; it could have been a thought, a prayer or even through curiosity. However, the request came about. You, my beloved, were synchronised to receive their request or called with divine intervention. The chills, the yawns, the cough, the burps, or the popping sounds are all expulsions of built-up energy released by the healer.

Every human being has been born with healing abilities. It is what one does with it that determines whether one will pursue this or whether one will be called upon to assist Spirit. For you are dictated by your soul group, as well as your elevation to the greater source. Any human can heal themselves and others. The difference is the passion, compassion and deep desire to help the soul's recovery so that they may live a more fulfilling life.

There is so much hurt in the world, whether it is psychological, physical or spiritual. All those beautiful souls that have been taken advantage of, it saddens me. We look everywhere for someone to help us as we battle issues that we find overwhelming to deal with. Sometimes, people don't know they need healing because their trauma has become so ingrained it has become part of who they are.

We search for the healer to mend our broken hearts. Personally, pharmaceutical drugs only seem to put a band-aid over the real problem. Because we don't know any better and think these large companies can cure us because "it says so in the advertisements and the media". The doctors push for these drugs as well. Alternative medicines have been around for centuries, and yet society disregards them in favour of the colossal drug lords.

Money-making entities suck the life out of human beings and help to end their lives or prolong them with drugs and feeding tubes, trapped within an endless loop of dependency. The market is now flooded with all sorts of healers and medicine doctors who claim to do wonders for your soul. Some I have never heard of before; that does not mean it is non-effective; it means I have not been exposed to that particular modality of healing. So, we search for our healer who helps us on the path that we want to go through discovery. There is no right or wrong way to choose how your body is healed; if conventional medicine is what you seek, by all means, let it be. Be patient and know that healing doesn't magically happen overnight. We live on a quick-fix planet, and most of us have no patience to persevere. Whoever you choose to help heal you, I pray that you find the right one for you. No judgement, of course, each to their own.

There is a new wave of healing at this time. The healing will, in time, help everyone to heal themselves. At the moment, humans may not be ready for the message to be given. Today, many humans have been indoctrinated, manipulated and conditioned to believe that they need a physician to help them with their ailments. Humans need to awaken and start to listen and understand that a physician is not the only option. When you listen to your temple (the body), it speaks loud and clear, but very few listen until the body screams or signals through pain receptors. Unfortunately for some, by that stage, it is too late.

Touch is not necessary in the new way of healing. Use the tips of your fingers to manipulate energy and currents; feel them through the tips of your fingers like electric pulses. Please understand that while working with currents, frequency and energy, you need to know how high the voltage needs to be to disperse into a patient or send out. Different people have different waves of energy, gentle does it at first so the body gets used to the energy surge and work up to another frequency.

Ask and we can guide you through this process. Feel and see the body, take note of the meridian lines. Reiki is very gentle at the beginning of a healing session, which will awaken the senses.

Scribe: Do you think we can heal ourselves?

Of course, Dear One, you have all the qualities that I have. Was man not made in the image of God? Then why does it seem so difficult? Awaken to your potential, awaken and know that ye are God and we are one of the same.

> *When the healer walks upon the Earth*
> *bringing light, darkness disappears.*

Eternity

We are eternal; it is our body that dies and goes back to the earth. We have lived amongst the galaxy and stars through past lives. We roam and become any element we want to experience when we leave this Earth. We are consciousness, a thriving part of The Creator that never ends. Our main goal is to learn and love unconditionally and to share our findings with others who struggle with life and living. Be confident about what you do in this lifetime, for you only get this life.

Do your best; I am sure that if you had a choice, you would not like to come back to Earth to repeat your lessons. Otherwise, you stay in kindergarten until you graduate to middle school. It may take many years for you to get through preschool, so please take your time and get it right the first time around. The Creator is eternal and omnipresent, and so are we, the eternal beings. Learning and experiencing everything, absorbing and creating new ideas for generations to come.

Our soul never ages; it has too many experiences to endure while on Earth. Even though the human body ages, you will hear older people state that they do not feel old until they see themselves in the mirror. You are only as old as you feel. We are equipped to slow the ageing process down, yet we still fuel our bodies with poisons.

> *You are a timeless soul of unconditional love.*

Evolution

There are a multitude of species changing and evolving over time, not only physically but mentally as well, giving them the ability to blend in well. Scientists believe we were born of apes and then began to evolve over centuries; in my opinion, I think this is so wrong. Although we may share similar characteristics, we are not of this species. Now I agree that coming from the ocean as a single-celled organism seems more believable because human babies live for nine months in water and are created from the combination of two single cells. Be who you are or evolve into what you are. You have finally remembered, so accelerate your higher purpose to help evolve into yourself and embrace it all.

> *Over time, we evolve emotionally, physically and mentally through our own experiences.*

Expansion

The more we expand our knowledge and worldview, the more we begin to initiate the light within us. The spark that lights the room when we enter, and the energy that resides within us, radiates love, allowing it to brighten someone's day. The very thought of coming together as a collective to unite as one is a sheer wonderment within itself. How can one do this when we have so many individual traits and personalities? Surround yourself with like-minded people, and from there, the world is your oyster.

That is what we are here to do: expand our ways of thinking and doing and remind ourselves that life is to be lived without regrets. The short life that we have on the planet is to be filled with everything and anything that you wanted to achieve. I believe it is never too late to chase your dreams and become who you want to be.

Life is given to you for a reason. So many are taken so early; their life never really began, so you are privileged to be here. Make the most of what you have and expand your horizons. If you can't do anything for yourself, do something for someone else. I am sure everyone needs a friend to help them on their journey. The pathway to freedom is knowledge and education. One can allow oneself to expand one's creativity and bring forth one's artistic abilities. There is so much wasted talent out there. We just need everything to be exposed and bought out into the open to share experiences and to be a mentor for those who may be a little lost.

If we are given options, we can go a long way in our lives. Show me, and I can do more. Walk with me, and I remain unstoppable! Lao Tsu said, 'Give a man a fish, and he will eat for a day, teach him how to fish and he will eat for a lifetime'. The same principle applies here.

Learn to love yourself more and to love what you do. We are but a speck in a mighty ocean of people. Expand your wisdom, and all else will follow. The years disappear quickly, so please don't wait for 'someday'. That day is today. The Universe holds you in high esteem. And you only need to ask. Be specific in your request, that is the only rule. Lift the vibration of your consciousness to meet the frequency of your soul.

Open your mind to all possibilities. The Universe calls you to accountability.

Expression

In the pages of my mind, I step forth and believe what I'm doing is right for me. I embrace all possibilities and creative ideas that come my way.

I am free to express how I feel, and I love beyond time and space. You are everything to me and always will be. You give me everything I need, and I am truly grateful. I reach toward Heaven and allow the cascading rain upon my face, which cleanses the drudgery of the day away. Then I may carry on with my daily life and live in harmony with myself and everything around me. Life is beautiful and I am grateful to be part of it right now. The experiences I've encountered along the way have been just a blessing. Lessons learned have brought me to where I am today. I have met some amazing people on this journey, and am in love with the whole process of giving and receiving love.

To express oneself verbally, written or otherwise, will give you the opportunity to say what you feel is authentic and right for you. Others express themselves through dance, art, poetry and so on. They share their passion with others, and we are delighted to be entertained by great works of life. Theatre is a wonderful expression of the arts; it shows our history and fantasy of far-off lands that may or may not have existed. It soon takes your mind, body and soul back to a lifetime that was forgotten. Children have a great way of expressing themselves through tantrums, which sometimes makes it awkward for parents at the supermarket. Patience teaches you to control yourself when you are under such duress. I feel for the parents when they are faced with this challenge.

How you express yourself seems to determine the individual you are. Lately, human beings have become quite controlled, and it seems you no longer have freedom to speak out about how you feel. You express yourself by protesting in the streets. It hasn't made a huge difference to the way people have been treated; there is a division now between us and them. There is no justice for those who force others to conform to what they want.

Have we become a liability to our country? What do we owe to the societal changes that are currently taking place? I am not sure, but I do know we have become puppets in a game of tug of war, us against them and ridiculed by a society that is supposed to support us and care what we do. But none of this is true anymore. The integrity has disappeared, and we are all alone to battle for ourselves against an entity that is far bigger than you or me. I am sure the future will look a little brighter as the years roll on. I still feel blessed to live in a country that supports those less fortunate where they can. The Creator sent me to Earth for a reason, and that reason has become apparent in the last couple of years, so I accept and take up the challenge.

Feel free to express yourself, anyhow and anywhere, with respect, of course. Be as loud as you like, freedom of speech should be willingly exercised and you are given the permission to do so. We are fortunate that we come from countries that allow freedom of speech.

Let everyone around you express themselves to be as free as they want to be. Learn to detach from negative energy.

Extraterrestrials

'Little green men', as humans call them, arrived on Earth before humans were seeded. They are scouts that monitor the earth; human beings claim to have been abducted by aliens. The beings that 'abduct' humans are not galactic; they are of their own planetary system, and they have come to study us. We do not interfere with their knowledge or why they are here.

'The silver ones,' as we will call them, are seen as cultivators; as one cultivates the land, so do the silver beings cultivate and manipulate humans. They are harmless. As you know, there is no such thing as the devil, for we all have choices.

The silver people came to show humans how to regenerate their own bodies. The Creator has sent them to assist mankind and help them understand themselves. Many beings throughout the Universe share the

Earth. So below and as above, there is a huge list of beings, who are also called aliens, visiting this planet. We are all caretakers and visitors, for no one owns her or ever will.

Scribe: There is a lot of hype at the moment about the ETs all over Facebook and the media stirring things up.

This is not new; conspiracy theories are doing their rounds again, making human beings afraid of the unknown. It is part of your history, of who you truly are, only you have forgotten. You have come from different planetary solar systems during your evolutionary state of being. It has been around for thousands of years, yet you're still in awe of what belongs to you. You really are asleep, aren't you? Wake up! See it for what it really is.

Scribe: What might that be?

To be in touch with your true selves and apply the new technology. Acknowledging that you, too, are termed a creature from another planet called Earth. Imagine how that feels to know the truth about yourselves and how brutal you can be to each other and yet also be so kind and loving as well. Every individual has a choice, and that has been gifted to you all for free by the Divine creator of all. You are born of His imagination and created to live a life as best you can without instructions, but to choose who and what you want to become.

Few galactic beings choose to destroy themselves as much as human beings... and they blame aliens for abduction! Did you ever think they may want to save the human race through abduction and not suck their brains out as what has been portrayed for so long? These are all scare tactics, and you believe everything you read, watch on media, or the gossip you hear from strangers in the street but never consult your own integrity to uncover the truth at face value.

Awaken to your past because that is what aliens are – your true ancestors. You are no different; they are just more advanced.

We need to listen with respect to those who may have encountered beings from other planetary systems and let them know there is no shame in what they have experienced. Those who have been abducted do not gain anything from telling their story; if anything, they would be ridiculed, medicated, and put away somewhere. ET intervention has forever been documented throughout our history, especially in indigenous cultures. They speak of ET visiting and the teachings on how to grow food and live on Earth respecting the resources.

Astrological teachings and ethnological advancement in artificial intelligence were among those philosophies. Many encounters were documented throughout the ages of mankind. A narrative of mythology has been depicted within many Native American cultures, South Africa, Myan, and Zulu, just to name a few. They will tell you of the planet where there was ET that came to Earth to teach and give us the building blocks of civilisation. These are all from the book of Enoch, the teachings that have been eliminated from the Bible.

There were also stories about women being abducted and impregnated, giving birth to giants called Nephilim in the Bible; the Greeks called them Titans. The mythological creatures of half man and half beast no longer seem to be mythological creatures. There is so much evidence that tells of giants and star people everywhere and in most countries, as documented in drawings on cave walls and statues depicting such tales.

What was the reason for making this taboo and keeping all of this hidden and not included in the Bible? We are now entering an era where all the secrets are being revealed. We are becoming more aware than ever about what actually happened to humanity. Most indigenous cultures have known of the encounters for many centuries and have continued to respect and nurture them, but modern religions do their best to hide them. Believe it or not, these things happened. We have only been given a portion of our knowledge of existence.

Scribed by Nita Jane

Scribe: What other life forms exist, and where do they reside?

Dear One, you have spent many lifetimes in numerous places. Life forms exist everywhere, right down to the particles that are airborne – they too exist on what they would deem a planet, whether it be your skin or perhaps your hair follicles. We are one big, massive movement, depending on where we reside. Where would you like to go? What would you like to see? Name your planet of choice; you have been there in one of your lifetimes. No matter what planet it was, the question would be, what kind of experience did you take away from the form that you decided to incarnate into? For they are all the same regardless of what civilisation you were in.

Some are primitive, others are advanced. Was it technology you gained from a previous life form? Was it pre-historic? All you need to ask is, "Why did I choose to reincarnate there? What did I learn? What have I carried into this lifetime?"

Is there a recurring pattern of behaviour that you cannot understand? If you still hold the technology from an advanced colony, maybe your frustration is not knowing how to communicate your findings here on Earth. What details do you specifically want to know about yourself from those 'Galaxy lifetimes?' I'm sure you find this fascinating but know that those lifetimes and your lifetimes here on Earth run along the same principle.

The advanced beings have learned not to war with each other, they have learned what hatred can do, they have learned environmental issues, and they have learned how to harness fossil fuels. Everything is shared; there is no suffering, only advancement. No one is higher or lower in status, religion, politics, or hierarchy.

Awaken to the reflection of your ancestors.

Fairies

The keepers of the forests, the beautiful wee folk created specifically to tend the gardens of The Creator. Human beings will see them when they want to be seen. They are mischievous, and some would say they are clever as well. They have to be, for human beings seek them out and destroy their habitat. There are folktales told about these creatures, and all are true. They were given the magical powers to survive. Human beings cannot be reborn into one of these creatures, although some find a magnetic pull toward them and resonate. Some human beings have stated that their past lives were of the fairy folk. That is because the fairies want you to experience a wee bit of their lives.

They are the tricksters of the earth and will do anything to protect their territory. They will not let you see them in full form, even though human beings may say they have encountered them. They may enter a home, and you will see them at the corner of your eye, only for them to disappear when you turn your head for a better look. What you see is what you see; don't doubt yourself. They love to play games.

Scribe: Are they like nymphs and other little beings? Why were they created?

All beings were created to live in peace and harmony. As human beings were created with the spark of the Divine, these little creatures were created to look after the forests, fauna, and flora. They all belong to the fairy realm, which is indeed real.

Human beings have been gifted with the spark of the Divine and choose not to use their abilities, preferring to stay locked within themselves, blaming environmental and social issues for their misery. Truth be told, human beings are of their own destruction.

An array of beings inhabit this earth alongside human beings; they know their place in the order of all things and know what's required. Human beings, however, disrupt the balance and interfere with other beings. Yes, I understand human beings are very inquisitive; however, instead of getting over their curiosity by simply acknowledging the creatures, they pursue them, examine them and try to assimilate these creatures, turning them into mini human beings, or worse, kill them in the process. Look at what human beings do to animals, dress them in human clothing, especially monkeys and dogs, and abuse them while performing tricks for entertainment. Let them be; animals would not do that to you.

Ask the fairies to guide the way;
they love unconditionally.

Faith

With greatness comes the knowing – knowing that all is well within your realm and within your thinking. The ability to see beyond the physical aspect of a human being. To be able to see the true person that resides within. Incredible beings have achieved such wonderful feats.

We all live in a simulated consciousness; *The Matrix* movie is a good example of this. Incredible studies have shown quantum parallel universes out there. It's enough to confuse the mind. Victory comes from those who recognise the patterns occurring within themselves.

Scribe: You're talking in riddles now; it's hard to keep up with what you are referring to; please explain?

As a human being, it is very hard for one to understand why you are here in the first instance; some will seek that, others will not be bothered and keep living life the only way they know how, or, they become conditioned to think there is no other way but to accept what has been handed to them. For better words, accepting of what's been 'dished out'.

Some will seek their existence normally through God, Christ and the Holy Spirit, depending on what culture you're coming from. Unfortunately, the Christian faith infiltrated the majority of indigenous cultures and turned them away from what was right for them. They were already in tune with the Divine and did not need to learn from a book that told lies and crippled so many nations. The *Bible* was not the problem, but the humans who administered the messages were not of sound mind or soul.

The darkness took hold of the *Bible* quite quickly, and the horrific history of assault ran rampant through all manner of Catholic-based institutions. And that's what they were; institutions. If it were anything to do with God, this is not what He would have wanted for his people.

Scribe: Why did the Divine allow that to happen?

Dear One, it was for all to awaken into the truth; unfortunately many suffered at the hands of some very sick individuals. Slowly they are being made accountable for what they have done. They, too, were only the Messengers and specifically agreed to come and fulfil this role as a soul experience.

If you look at soul experiences rather than anything else that can be formulated in your mind, you will begin to see a bigger picture and understand that you all have come to Earth to fulfil your desired soul experience; no one or nothing has forced you. Your soul has asked to experience something specific in order to ascend to the next level of your evolution. You all signed a contract before coming to Earth, and life happened. We know how hard it is to understand, coming from a human perspective, the horrific stories you hear each day.

We are not saying that you could become desensitised from it all. We are saying that you each have a role to play, so begin to play it well. You experience life for your soul to learn, so you may return home one day and realise you have mastered the next step in your soul elevation. For you do not want to keep repeating the same drama over and over again and not learn anything.

The question you must ask yourself is, "What have I learned from this life experience and how can I stop repeating the same pattern?" While you are going through this, you must be gentle on yourself.

> *You are the ray of sunshine*
> *that glows in the dark.*
> *You are the love that captured my heart.*
> *You are the soft sound I hear everywhere,*
> *and the jingle of bells I know in my ears.*
> *You are the vision I saw in my dreams.*
> *You are the Divine that is so supreme.*

Family

Your family is your backbone; others will come and go, for you are all the same in essence. Learn to uplift each other in love, peace and understanding. For when one aligns with The Creator, you will all follow, whether consciously or unconsciously, for the rest will not or may not understand what is happening. We call it clustering as the stars are in the skies. You will group together, which is what you currently do, for you feel most comfortable with your own like-minded souls. This is why you have been brought together as a family!

We do not always agree with what our family says or does. But you know that if anything happens, they will be there to support you. Family doesn't have to be genetically linked, either. You choose your family by selecting which friends to bring into your inner circle.

Family forgive and forgets easily. Your galactic family are always around and will never leave. The Angels and Messengers are part of you, but others may not believe that they exist. For the Lord, thy God loves us so much he sent his only son so that he who believes in Him shall have everlasting life.

Dear One, you are from a long line of seers who have worked with us for many Millennia. It is as natural to you as drawing breath. In this lifetime, somehow, your natural abilities were suppressed. This is who you really are.

We are here to encourage you to seek out others like yourself, gather together, and support each other, for this is where you will also find your strength, as in the ability to move forward with your writings. Do not be perturbed by what is and what is not. Failure to reach others through your writings will indeed be a loss to all who seek the Divine. The omnipresence seeks the wisdom of the one you know, the one we have chosen. Ultimate sacrifice now, all is to be perfectly timed, for the Divine has orchestrated as such.

Dear One we, The Collective, will be here to support you anyway we can. Ask and ye shall be given.

Give thanks and gratitude for all you receive and all those who are in your life right now.

Fear

As day turns into night and the stars come out and align with the cosmos, the earth adjusts itself as the moon orbits the Earth, and has done so for millions of years. The Moon has various names from all cultures. The moon has witnessed all manner of the afflictions upon Man, from War to natural disasters, diseases and so forth. Yet, the human being still manages to survive after thousands of years. Marama - the name given to the moon in Māori - one who has seen everything that human beings have done and occupied spaces where humans were not meant to survive. We can live and survive anywhere as well; we are very adaptable creatures. Our offspring seem to become resilient to anything, and our DNA changes over time, and we adapt really well. There is so much to learn about ourselves, and our capabilities seem endless. We can do all things through faith. Sometimes, we live our lives in fear. Fear of the unknown, physically and spiritually. Call it what it is, but at the end of the day, we need to learn how to embrace our fears and face them head-on. Deal with them and move on; brave is the person who challenges the fear and overcomes it all. You can do it. We know you can.

Fear not, for I am with thee! Do not be afraid and close off from the world; the world needs you. Anything could spark fear. It is not a weakness and is a common human reaction to anything unfamiliar. Millions suffer from this debilitating emotion. It can push people into a dark place, so dark that there seems to be no escape from it. Where it started is anyone's guess, but it normally stems from childhood trauma.

No one can tell you to get over it because it seems so real, and it is for some. Fear may develop into a physical ailment as well. There are professionals out there who can help. Many people find as they get older, they have become bolder and don't give a sh*t about what anyone thinks anymore. When you finally overcome labels and have let go of meeting the expectations of others, your life begins, and you will feel alive.

You live in a world of fascination; do not be afraid to experience it all. If you don't step out of your comfort zone, you will miss so many opportunities along the way. Don't deprive yourself of a better existence. It's all waiting for you!

Be brave enough to give it a go, Dear One! We have faith that you can overcome this, and we know you can do it! In God's love, we leave you.

> *Conquer your fears and arrive*
> *at your destination quicker.*

Feminine energy

Elohim is another name for God and is frequently used in the Hebrew bible. When I first encountered Elohim, I saw a beautiful female dressed in a light blue chiffon flowing gown. I had no idea what or who this was, and I was not familiar with the name Elohim either.

"Who are you?" I asked. The answer came back, "I am neither male nor female; I come from the Source, and you see me the way you want to. I will always come dressed as you see me now as a female of femininity. For you are more comfortable speaking to the feminine energy when asking questions about female affairs."

Elohim: I am here. I come with love and compassion for humanity with peace and glory for mankind.

The feminine entity of all women shrouded in respect and ambience for the flame that flickers within her will never burn out; the loins of our existence are birthed within ourselves. Reach down and pluck the petal, Dear One, for you hold in your hands the key to all of humanity the birth of new life that flows like a river, through torrents that quicken. Hear my voice, the voice of the Angels. Know the feminine strength is like no other.

We are the leaders of tomorrow. We share the same earth, mother energy; we give life, we take life. We are all that hold man together. We are soft and gentle, and yet we are also strong and self-confident. Our qualities as warriors have linked us through the ages. My divine daughter, the warrior spirit dwells deep within you, and you have carried the weight of the male energy on your shoulders for too long. We ask the feminine energy to release the burden from you now, for you have had to be the male and the female to raise your children; there has been an imbalance. We now help you to rebalance yourself in order to experience the feminine side of who you are.

Let us acknowledge that you were once your father's son in another lifetime. This is something you had to experience, however you nurtured this throughout your life, which gave you a masculine persona. Dear beloved child of mine, I have come today to help you to realign your male/female energy.

Scribe: How do I do that? Does it require some sort of ritual?

No, it means you are not the father to your children; you are their mother. What would a mother do? You no longer need a tough exterior to intimidate or protect like a lion.

Scribe: But I am the protector of this family; I have no male influence.

You are the female energy; you are not the male. We will help you to balance so that you are more feminine. Indulge yourself more in womanly affairs.

Scribe: I don't know what you mean.

You have forgotten what it means to be female.

Scribe: I agree. I don't know what that includes or how I need to change to see myself as more feminine. Through my eyes, I see the feminine as physically weak.

That is not so; look back on your history, and you will see mighty examples of feminine strength. The strength to be feminine does not necessarily mean physical strength, for a woman can outwit a male - hands down. Yes, I understand you have never encountered a male who was able to be a mentor to your children, so you had to step in to be both mother and father, even to your sons; it is time for you now. Time to let go of trying to be both. Time to be you, are you ready?

Scribe: Yes. As I close my eyes, the beautiful Elohim takes me by the hand and leads me to the beautiful blue ocean. I witness the blue of the sea, the white surf rolling in and out off the sparkling sand and the beautiful warm sun on my face. Elohim sits and holds both my hands and whispers while we both look out to the ocean, and there is a sigh of relief. "Gently let go, Dear One, you are whole again. Do not fear your femininity." While still holding hands on the sandy embankment overlooking the rolling waves, a flood of tears is released, and I am whole. The beautiful Elohim embraces me as a mother would a child.

So, to all you beautiful women out there who need to recapture their femininity. I take your hand right now and lead you to a safe place where you can be the feminine, beautiful soul that you are.

The balance within each human being is the flow of both feminine and masculine energy equally and is so important to everyone. Sometimes, we come to earth with the wrong bodies that do not fit the internal functions of our bodies. We try to live the best we can in a body that does not seem to belong to us, which is pure hell for some trying to fit into a society that is not accepting of our choices in life.

Some were born female, yet they resonate with male energy and vice versa. We come to earth lifetime after lifetime, either as male or female.

Sometimes, the crossover gets a little confusing, and we are stuck within two sexes, male and female combined. Historically, we had to choose, but now it is becoming more acceptable to maintain our organs rather than have them removed so that you are one or the other gender. You were born both for a reason, a very unique brand of superhuman being. You have to be super balanced to live in a world that ridicules those who are different. Native cultures did not discriminate against those who felt they were born in the wrong bodies. They were actually cherished and embraced because they walked in two worlds.

> *Embrace who you are, and don't let anyone tell you otherwise.*

Fight or flight

Listen to your gut feeling and what it is telling you. Have you arrived at a point in your life where you're now listening to your intuition? That is a response everyone should be in tune with. When your intuition tells you not to *go there*, listen. It is part of your instinct from years of human evolution. The fight or flight mode. Human beings need something to alert them of dangerous situations, and this is where your intuition kicks in. I'm sure you have been in a situation where you feel very uncomfortable; your intuition is telling you to get out of there or suffer the consequences.

There are many examples of people using their intuition when a situation does not seem right. Turning right instead of left has avoided me being stuck in a traffic jam. Leaving a little later because I lost my keys, I have avoided a car pileup or accident. Being in the right space at the right time and that gut feeling can send chills down your back and on your arms as confirmation. You could be speaking to a person who appears to be nice, but your intuition is showing you something else. The hair on the back of your neck will stand up.

These feelings we have are there to protect us from outside influences. Body language is the same. If you don't like the way someone is gesturing or moving in a certain way, move yourself away from them; the energy they possess does not resonate with your own energy.

What you know is right for you; do not question your intuition.

Flow

Let it flow – the tears, the water and the stream of love. Steady as she goes, free falling from the top of the mountainside down to the depths of the ocean and back into the beautiful blue skies. Energy is all around us, flowing back and forth, sending all the glorious vibes out, and giving life to everything that's in its path. As the creative flow of miracles trickle down the mountain, the water is as cold as ice as it reaches the next town through the valley, bursting forth while renewing plant life, bringing a much-needed deluge of precious abundance.

When you understand the rules of the game. You become the creator of your own experiences.

Forgiveness

Start to forgive yourself. What you thought was the best thing to do at the time may not have been. It is too late to stop whatever it was; what happened, happened. Do not feel guilty about the situation. Decisions were made and followed through. Forgive the other person who has hurt you. There is no need to carry the baggage around with you. Drop the baggage, and do not let it live in your space and occupy your thoughts.

Your freedom from all of this is one thing you need to be mindful of. You exercised your freedom and your rights, so please, let things go and love yourself more. Know you are perfect in every way. There were no mistakes, and all is well. Learn from everything you do. Experience tells us that we will not do the same thing again, although some people are devils for punishment and keep going back for more. Sad, but so true. If you are in that pattern, forgive yourself and learn, and you can move forward to a much more fulfilling life.

> *Forgive those who have wronged or hurt you, for in doing so, you release the energy that wasn't meant for you. It belongs to them; let them own it.*

Foundation

What is your foundation and what makes you hold it together? I can only speak from experience and tell you that my foundation is my family. They represent to me the support that I need in order to get to where I am going. They are brutally honest when you want to know the truth about something you have done or you're about to do that does not fit or sit well with the paradigms of how we were raised. They will kick your arse and tell you not to be disrespectful to yourself. So, laying a solid foundation is very important in this lifetime; it helps you to find balance in all things. One without foundation is one without stability. Friendships and network systems are also a great way of building a solid relationship and a fundamental foundation. To love and to be loved is something we search for, sometimes our whole lives. This is also what makes a wonderful base and foundation awesome!

"Therefore, everyone who hears these words of mine and puts them into practice is like a wise man who built his house on the rock."
– Matthew 7:24-27

Freedom

To all the servicemen and women who fought for our freedom, we are so grateful and appreciate the sacrifice you gave in order for us to become free citizens of our country. I thank you, and the world thanks you. So many young men and women did not get to have a family of their own or experience their first true love. Gone too soon. Rest in peace, brave soldiers.

We can be free from ourselves as well after we fight demons that seem to consume our every waking moment. Thank goodness there are professionals out there to help us along with our walk through life because all we want is some kind of normality and freedom to express ourselves in a world that is becoming controlled by those who think it is their right to take away our freedom.

It is sad to think we have come this far, and yet we have learned nothing about humanity. How much we dishonour those who fought for our freedom only to turn our backs on them when they come back from the war. We should hang our heads in shame to think they gave their lives for nothing. I am glad my father is not here to witness any of it.

I pay tribute and honour to those who fought in World War II, Māori Battalion C Company, also nicknamed the 'Cowboys', was built from East Coast tribes from Tōrere around East Cape through Gisborne and over to Muriwai.[1] The membership included Ngāitai, Te Whānau-ā-Apanui, Ngāti

---

[1] Dr Monty Soutar, *Ngā Tama Toa: The Price of Citizenship.* David Bateman, 2008.

Porou, Te Aitanga a Hauiti, Rongowhakaata, Te Aitanga-a-Mahāki and Ngāi Tāmanuhiri. Their bravery, along with my father, will not be forgotten.

For our future, all children should have the freedom to express themselves and to live in a world where we celebrate the children and their creativity and ideas, for we older generation have run our course and we can teach our young ones what we learned if they choose to listen. We should be supporting all of them the best we know how sharing our wisdom and unconditional love. That is all children want these days: someone to listen to them and to feel safe and secure.

Having the right equipment in order for it to make things flow better is well worthwhile. Freedom is a word used lightly but can mean so much when you think of a bird and the way it drifts on the wind with no care in the world, the way it glides in mid-air. Human beings long to be like that bird. They always say, "Oh wow, I wish I could fly!" That is exactly where you go in your dream state, through meditation and while you sleep at night. Over the mountain through the trees souring high above the clouds and by the sea, moving faster above the sea, skimming the surface as you smell the sea air, hovering for just a minute over the sandy shore. And morning arrives, and you awaken from your slumber.

I have the freedom to be who I want to be. I choose my life and create it from my heart.

Free will

We all have free will and choices to make. We were born that way. The freedom to think outside the box and never have to be accountable to anyone. We live in a society that encourages free will. Look around at the children; they are not held accountable for anything. They basically do what they want with no consequences. However, they are the next generation of adults that will take over. It has been the norm now to speak up and tell the world what you want and what you think; soon, the political arena will be run by children who no longer want to live in a society run by stiff-necked politicians dictating and getting nowhere, making false promises. The children today are tired of that old paradigm of thinking.

Renewal is rampant at this time, and people will work together in harmony to build a new future for the next generation. Lo and behold all things will come to fruition. There will be no drought nor hunger, and the nations will unite to bring peace and equilibrium back upon the Earth. Verily, I say unto you, I am blessed to be alive to witness the upheaval. The old doctrines will fall away, making way for the new ways of doing and thinking. Time on the Earth is precious. We need to make sure that we live up to our end of the bargain and look after Mother Earth so we can live in a sustainable environment.

Our bodies are not here that long and are deteriorating day by day. We pollute the spaces we live in yet expect to be healthy. Don't fall for the advertisements giving you false hopes. Research and find another way to participate in society. Get the right answer from an honest source because most businesses just want your money and can't provide the services you are looking for. It is very hard to find genuine people today, ones who want the best for you without trying to scam or get as much money as they can from you. The search goes on until there is divine intervention and synchronicity occurs.

Follow your own guidance; don't let go of your plans and dreams, and don't allow them to be crushed by the opinion of others.

Full moon

Dear One, the cosmos is realigning itself to become a beacon of strength to all those who are able to harness the energy of the full moon.

Scribe: Is there a ritual around what we should be doing at this time?

No. Bask in the energy of the moon. She will bring you clarity and personal growth with love and great respect. Know that within you everything is from the brilliance of the Source. The energy that aligns with the moon also signals a shift within your human body.

So, think of the synchronicity that occurs within; it would be a perfect time to release old hurts and develop love for oneself, reprogram your body, mind and soul, and figure out what you would like for yourself. Many roads you have travelled, Dear One. You have now entered the crossroads to success. You will now be guided through to the next stages in your life. Embrace it all; time waits for no one.

Scribe: What do you think the future holds?

Dear One, the future brings with it a new wave of doing things perfectly with love and balance. Expertise in specific fields will multiply to enrich human existence on the planet.

Human beings will become a lot friendlier, less stressed and more pleasant to be around. Strength in numbers will be the flavour of the day as it brings in great support networks that help to develop stronger ties. Enhancement in daily living will become normalised as your economy starts to straighten itself out. Better government systems will be put in place as old ones crumble to the wayside, no longer being able to sustain untruthful practices. This will make it easier for human beings to survive and live happier and fruitful lives.

Do not buy into the fact that man will fall, for we have dictated the end, and it is not near. The human race will continue but will get better as their understanding of spiritual practices and life itself is embraced rather than being seen as a phenomenon or something only a few human beings are capable of. Tens of thousands will awaken at once and take up the ideology.

Scribe: There have been so many yellow and black wasps outside my house. Apart from being scary in a swarm, what could possibly be the spiritual significance of such a thing?

Dear One, apart from the fact that they, too, seek refuge out of the heat, they also seek the light that shines so bright from your home.

They have come to support your journey by uplifting the vibration with their wings vibrating at a rapid pace. They have been sent as Messengers. So, Dear One, we ask that you leave them and avoid them, as they will leave of their own accord when their mission is complete. It is also a symbol of wealth, good luck and prosperity.

Scribe: The bee is seen as a symbol of Jesus Christ's attributes. The honey reflects his sweet and gentle character, while the sting pertains to justice and the cross. I did not understand the spiritual significance, and I am ignorant.

My beloved child of the Universe, it brings us great pleasure to bring you the information you require to bring truth to a subject and to help those we recognise as having many difficulties and struggles in their lives. If we are able to bring relief to a certain area in one's life, that is granted. To overcome such hardships, we are never far away; as you know, we are part of you.

Scribe: Every day, I am in awe of the accuracy and love I feel from you all. Everyone else can feel your resonating unconditional love as well, and it does not matter where I am. The many blessings I receive are overwhelming and beautiful. You have given me patience, love, clarity, and a deeper understanding of who and what I am. The amazing thing is I am not tired. I feel a glow of tremendous love.

Only radiating love and gratitude will forever be etched in you. Be more observant and aware, wake up and look at your surroundings. Everything is alive. Attune yourself to all that surrounds you.

Make the effort to dream big.

Future

You are the ancient words of wisdom. The children of today are our future. They will be here when we have left to go on our next journey. We must leave them with the right tools to equip them with self-esteem, self-love and care for the environment. And, most of all, they should believe in themselves. I write these words because I need to know before I leave that all people – and most of all, our children – are left with tools to help them find themselves and their purpose in life.

It is useless to try to tell the child, "You're good at this". Children need to figure this out for themselves. The children now are very advanced individuals. The key to a well-balanced child is self-love, and they need to be comfortable in their own skin to nurture what is already there and to find their true calling. We are all born with talent and gifts, whether you have been raised in a dysfunctional environment or not – even when bullies have torn you down to a state where you find yourself no longer able to get up and fight the demons. They won't go away unless we confront them, and then they run when the light shines in the dark.

*True success knows itself. Who are
you, and where are you going?*

Generations

Older people are so wise and have so many life experiences and stories to share. We forget that they were once young and able. I love how the older generations show us their amazing photographs of themselves as young people. It is great for the grandchildren to know a bit of history and genealogy about their past. Children are always fascinated by stories. At my age, I still love to hear them, whether it's fact or fiction. By listening to an older person reliving their past, you are giving them a great gift of memories and recalling an era that is long gone but remains concrete in their minds. What a wonderful way to express love. There is much we can be grateful for and learn from our parents and grandparents when they share their knowledge.

In turn, you will share with your own children and grandchildren. It is, without a doubt, the best gift ever. We forget so quickly how precious life is, and we flounder to try and make sense of it all. Giving an older person a gift is nice, but all they really want is for someone to listen because they know that the world around them is consumed with too much material commercialism.

I am light.

Geniuses

The beautiful people of the Universe, the Dear Ones who touch our hearts, the closeness they have to the Divine; the wonderful way they are. We send them to Earth to enlighten their families and friends around them. They are such a joy to behold. They are still with us but walk the planet Earth with other human beings. They enter this world for a reason; they teach human beings to love unconditionally, to love their deepest and to have patience.

They touch the hearts of whoever comes in contact with them, these forever-lighted beings, God's special children. For the light that glows from them is the love of the Lord. He shines through them like the precious jewels that they are. Chosen to be here in a form that cannot function by human standards. They function at the highest vibration and frequency of the Divine in perfect harmony with the Earth for they own the right in this world to be heard. Who are these wonderful beings? They have been identified by society and given diagnoses – autistic, Asperger's, Down syndrome, or classed as those with 'special needs'.

I know who I am. I am perfect in every way.

Give and receive

The more you give, the more you receive. It is all energy. When you give from the right intention and do not expect anything in return, the wheel of fortune spins in your favour. It is not only monetary giving that is important, but also giving your time to those who need your love, understanding and patience. It's not hard to spend time with someone who is lonely or with those who need comforting. We all need someone to tell us we are doing an amazing job. It raises our vibration and helps us to feel good about ourselves. The unconditional love you have for someone is real and genuine; it can be felt by the recipient easily. It is so easy to show interest in what everyone is doing or creating. So, strike up a conversation; you will never know what you may learn.

> *"Bring me sunshine in your smile.*
> *Bring me laughter all the while."*
> – Willie Nelson

Gratitude

Watch how the leaves fall, and the wind carries them away. The branches sway as the breeze whistles through the trees. The air is crisp, and the nostrils flare as we take a deep breath. We are truly blessed to be able to breathe fresh air. Our lungs fill and expand as we then exhale again. We close our eyes and thank the day. When we acknowledge that we will have a wonderful day, we will keep that positive frame of mind and smile at ourselves. Life will smile back at us.

Life is not supposed to be difficult; it is something that we have put upon ourselves. Find comfort in all that you do and say, and be kinder to you. Take a nice, long stroll along the pathway toward happiness. I don't know how people develop depression; all I know is it is real. Life is full of opportunities and community spirit. One just needs to seek and find like-minded folk. Believe and receive the greatest gift given unto you; life itself.

Make a list of gratitude for food, water, friendships, family, fun, good health, happiness, laughter, a new baby, having a wonderful job that you love. It is so easy and also comes naturally to you. There is an appreciation when wonderful people come into your life.

Fantastic happenings come into your life when you begin to appreciate anything and everything around you. Miracles start to happen, flowers bloom, the grass looks greener, and your eyes adjust to a clear lens that you can look through. The sky is clear, and the night skies are full of beautiful stars that twinkle in the night; shooting stars cross the galaxy and knock on the doors of the celestial beings. The night is filled with the sound of crickets, frogs and all manner of creatures, and I appreciate my eyesight and sharp hearing. The smells are amazing. The environment is absolutely incredible!

We must be grateful for all that we receive. Every day is a different day, but we must not forget that we have been given this day. Be grateful for the birds that fly through the air and deposit seeds everywhere. Be grateful for the bees pollinating the plants that we eat; the trees, fauna and flora for the oxygen and fruit they bear for us. Be grateful for all the wonderful people in our lives and for the ones who have come to bring us lessons. Thank you for the many blessings and miracles that have come our way. Relax a lot more and embrace the life you were given.

Celebrate the milestones in your life and never beckon your past. Try not to scratch at old wounds so they won't heal. Dissolve the past; it will not serve you in this lifetime. Concentrate on what lies before you and everything will turn out just fine. Have faith that you are more than capable of doing anything.

As the dawn breaks, my love remains with you. You are the light that brightens up the room. You are the love I see everywhere. Your truth and integrity are second to none. I see you, I feel you and I know who you are. I follow your path of righteousness. Thank you for believing me, and allowing me to be me. I seek answers to my many questions about life, and where to from here. They tell me it is no concern but to concentrate on living the best life that we were born to live. Make it happy, joyous and drama-free. Embrace wonderful people all around you, and make sure these are the only people in your space. You get what you attract, so make sure your whole demeanour is positive, judgement-free, loving, caring and compassionate. Love who you are, and love loves you back. Remember that you are the spark of the Divine and nothing less.

When you are grateful for all that you have and are, the Universe celebrates with you!

Growth

The tree spreads out her magical branches to nurture her children while protecting and giving them stability, for the roots remain anchored to the ground while there are struggles on the surface. She juggles many issues, manmade issues, for she has had to make sure her roots dig deep into the ground to bypass and avoid all the pollution within the air and soil.

She has had to adapt to protect her saplings. Life is like this; we can love and nurture our family all we like, but there are those who would like to take advantage of our kindness and loving ways, only to be poisoned with hostility. However, we keep an open mind, keep going, and do what we are doing, sending unconditional love to those who may want to harm us.

When sending love and compassion for others and expecting nothing in return, one can only know that they are supported by the highest vibration of love. The love is sent back tenfold, giving and receiving. But that's not all a carer does; she has the wisdom to know what is right and what is wrong and to repair all things that mothers naturally do. The fighter, the justice keeper, the nurse, the taxi driver, the warrior and above all, the teacher. My love and respect to all females and males who are the nurturers for the next generation.

You are a timeless being who grows and learns life's lessons.

Happiness

Everybody strives to be happy and to remain joyful, but it is not that easy for some, especially when you have come from a place of torment your whole life. How is it possible to feel these types of emotions? How do you create for yourself a safe place in order to get in touch with these emotions? Forgiving is a great place to start because it opens the gateway for bitterness to melt away and bring forth more positive ways of thinking and doing.

New concepts begin to emerge as you find a happier place to be in your mind. Don't let the demons of the past rule you; your life is yours and no one else's, so please do not let negative energy dictate your life. You are bigger and better than that. It is time for you to take up the challenge and only you can make that happen. Do what brings joy to your life – perhaps a new hobby or meeting with other people in your situation so you can heal the past together.

You have the potential to change your life if you want to; you just need faith and a will to do it. Nobody wants to stay trapped in a cage when there is so much to explore out there. We run the risk of lying down and never getting back up. We constantly belittle ourselves for not knowing enough, or being enough or trying to be like someone else. You are the perfect you, the unique individual brought to Earth for a reason. There is no one else like you. The wonderful, intelligent human being, God's child of the Universe. The abilities you have far exceed you, and your knowledge is boundless. Be happy and remain joyful. We love you.

> *The happiness you seek is within you.*
> *There is no need to look anywhere else.*

Harvest moon

Scribe: What is one required to do at this time?

Astrologists believe that the Earth and the moon move around the sun at precisely the right time.

Now, let's look at what you have done in the past year. Do you think you have made a difference to yourself, your family, your environment, or perhaps your inner being? If the answer is yes to all of these, you may harvest; this is an excellent time to reap what you have sown.

Whatever your intentions were for one whole Lunar Year, so shall you reap. According to Socrates' theory, cause and effect runs along the same axis. Make a list of where you may have improved or lacked, this you will reap. What you planted a year ago is ready to be harvested.

There is no ritual around this. All that is needed is pen and paper unless you have a diary or can produce a commentary on what you did for the whole year.

I have questions for you:

What kind of ideas did you have?
Were they to fulfil your desires or someone else's?
Think about how you could have handled this better!

Thank and bless the Lunar Year for all the lessons it has brought you. Be kind to yourself, please be loving, gentle and kind. The harvesting is the end; the fruits are bountiful. Depending on what was used as fuel to grow your garden, this will either be bountiful or very sparse. Dear One, this is a very good time to plant your seeds for the next lunar season. It is there that your next harvest will bloom with full colour and radiance.

Today is a day to celebrate. We love you and will never leave you. In peace and love.

We reap what we sow, Dear One.

Heaven

Scribe: What is the difference between Earth and Heaven?

They are of the same.

Scribe: Please explain.

The light reflects both in Heaven and Earth. What you see here is what you see in Heaven.

Scribe: Are you saying that it is an individual choice as to how you perceive things to be?

Yes, that is so. If you want to see Angels in Heaven and the God waiting with his arms stretched out, so be it. Heaven is the way one sees one's life to be and a reflection of one's worldview. It has been written that two or more looking at the same object will see two different things.

Take care with your thinking and doing and remember that you are now in the consciousness of the fifth dimension. Therefore there is no need to have three-dimensional thoughts; egoism, fear, blame, sadness, hate, anger and all of these attributes that no longer reside in this way of thinking. Please rise above it all.

Distance and time will not keep me from you.

Higher realm

Scribe: Father, explain to me what it's like to live in His realm.

Dearest One, you have come from the magnificence of my unconditional love where the rivers run deep and the oceans are blue, the mountains are tall and the grass is green, the moonlight is clear, and it's all for you, my dear.

Scribe: Sometimes I feel it is so hard to live here on Earth. The destruction and the hate. Even though it does not affect me directly, I feel for those who are going through such a hard time right now.

Of course, you will feel the effects of others because you are all connected to the one Source. Rise above the vibration that does not serve you. Embrace the love you have inside you, and move on a wave of understanding and empathy, for you cannot wallow in someone else's misery, otherwise, it distorts your own reason for being on Earth.

Put aside those past hurts that linger and embrace the now. Safeguard your feelings and heart so you may stay intact. Do not let your emotions undermine who you are.

Love is the only thing we take with us.

Higher self

Scribe: How do we connect to our higher self?

Dear One, do not get distracted easily, for we need you as much as you need us. Keep your focus with us and try not to be sidetracked for all the answers to your questions lie with us. Don't worry about what humans think or do; keep your eyes forward and focus on us. No matter what you have read and what you have seen on social media – be it known to you that our words are true and authentic.

We do not need an explanation; we come from a higher frequency of love and understanding. It is that part of a human that is connected to the Source therefore information is filtered through the pineal gland. The pineal gland is known as the third eye and serves as a connection between the physical and the spiritual worlds. Hence, the writings, more and more humans are becoming activated or are able to channel now.

It is becoming the 'norm.' We will rejoice when all humans listen to the better part of themselves, their higher self. It will mean no struggle, no more questions that make no sense to us. Frequently asked questions such as: Who are you? What do you want? And why are you here?

We, too, can ask that of you. What would be your answer to that? We are trying to explain who you really are, but you still interrogate us as though we have done something wrong. All we have done is answer your call. You can hang up on us anytime you like, but we know you will search for us again.

The dilemma that you face within yourself is not knowing whether you believe what has been written is not regurgitated from some other resource. We have written these same words before. Every human has access to our words. They may seem repetitive, but for those who want to know where they fit into the world as an individual, our words will find them through you, Dear One.

Too many resources discourage the seeker from finding us. They think you have to be a mystic in order to receive our teachings. That is not so. You, my Dear One, are loved and cherished by us. Ask your question, small or great; we have the answer.

The Body – has more than seventy-eight organs in total.

The Consciousness – has awareness, awake and involved.

The Unconsciousness – has no awareness, is asleep and seeks validation.

The Subconsciousness – has ideas and self-experiences. Left to marinate, holds on to past trauma.

The Semiconscious – in-between waking and asleep.

The Higher Self – loves above all, is unemotional, cares about all people, is non-judgemental, speaks with wisdom, celebrates achievements, embraces all, and does not find fault with anything or anybody. And above all, has freedom.

> *"Keep your face always toward the sunshine and shadows will fall behind you."*
> – Walt Whitman

Identity

Identity is indeed a strong word in today's society. What and who do you identify as? It doesn't matter for we have all come to Earth for one reason and that is to experience all we can in order to elevate ourselves onto the next journey in life.

You may identify as a grandparent, parent, or sibling or even identify yourself by your profession. Each identity holds significance but also expectations. Likewise, there may be ways in which other people define you: pretty or handsome, intelligent, talented, articulate, reliable. They are positive attributes but also carry the weight of expectation. Many of us grow up with negative labels; overweight, ugly, useless, stupid. These are often words given by people who are projecting their own unhappiness or insecurities onto you. You may know this in your heart, but that doesn't make the labels hurt any less. Learning to live with ourselves is hard enough without adding more labels.

Be confident in your own identity; you do not need to take on anything that doesn't belong to you energetically. You do not have to fit into any box that society creates for you. You are a child of God and brilliant in your own unique way.

Identity evolves as we do, shifting and changing to meet where we are in life and to reflect what we believe in.

Always stand up for what you believe is right for you. Everyone has free choice in this lifetime. Never be afraid to identify as the person you feel inside. When you embrace your authentic nature, you will truly shine.

Today I accept and love both the positive and negative aspects of myself.

Illumination

As darkness falls, the stars come out to play. The moon lights the way. The pathway is filled with fireflies and my love for you all the way. Criticise me not, love me for who I am. For the beacon that shines from my heart is for all. My body illuminates. The songs of the crickets can be heard as the undergrowth comes to life. Never be afraid of the dark. Walk in peace and show your stance, own your space. There is nothing that is willing to harm you, especially with the Lord walking alongside you.

Bathe in the cool, clear waters and embrace the feeling of oneness with the planet. Share your awareness with all who are willing to listen. Tell stories about the interconnectedness of all living beings and how we are one with all in our environment. Seek thee the kingdom of God, for it lies within all the magical beings that we are. We just need to know and believe it is so.

I am strong and fearless, and I am me; there is no other like me. I am brave, loving and kind. I am intelligent as well as the beautiful child of God. I can do all things possible because I believe and have no doubt about who I am.

There are days when I don't know what I am doing and wonder why I was chosen to write. I ask myself: "Why do I need to be the one to carry this load?" I realise it is a gift that has been placed before me, and it is a privilege to be able to carry this through to the next stage of my life.

To honour all the beings of light that reside and guide me every step of the way. So, I pick myself up and say, "Why not me? I can do this. I only need to focus". The more I focus, the clearer everything seems to be. At the end of the day, the words belong to the world, and I am grateful and thankful to be able to be part of the most incredible, creative piece of work that has ever been placed before me.

Far beyond sight and sound, there lies the truth of the ages. Something that holds secrets to the early lives of our ancestors carved in stone, preserved for all to know. My rights are the same; somewhere out there, they have been recorded on tablets, sealed for all time, and are now being respected by the scriber in this lifetime. Age has no meaning where Spirit dwell. The masters have all been ancient and carry with them wisdom of the ages that have passed through many generations. Dear One, you will pass into the afterlife with your talents still with you, and lifetime after lifetime, you will improve. Soon, you will use technology to bring forth the words to the next generations, for they are so important. To others, the words are inspiration and hope for the future.

> *"Darkness cannot drive out darkness; only light can do that. Hate cannot drive out hate; only love can do that."*
> – Martin Luther King Jr.

Inspiration

Watching others attain their goals is certainly inspiring, especially if you have witnessed the initial struggle from that person and they are advancing and meeting every milestone. What about you? How are you reaching your achievements and allowing yourself to invest in yourself? What is it that you're asking and wanting to do?

Inspiration not only comes from others; it comes from within. When you see something that sparks a memory or an invention is born, what inspired you to think about that in the first instance? We get ideas because we know we can do better to assist ourselves, so we create an easier solution. Like, for instance, the zipper in the trousers. Before zips, buttons were used to hold everything together. There are so many innovative ideas floating around, and they are all there for the taking. Because we are all one big consciousness, we all think as a collective, and we all have access to great ideas.

Find what inspires you. The spark inside grows stronger every day. You will have that lightbulb moment where you would like to share your inspiration with someone. We are here to listen!

> *"Creativity is intelligence having fun."*
> – Albert Einstein

Intuition

There is so little we know about ourselves. We search the globe for the right answer, which is usually right in front of us – or within us. There is a small sparrow within who wants to be free to fly off with the flock, but we find that we cannot resist the breadcrumbs, and we get caught in a trap by our own greed. The temptation is too great to see what we could have. We now watch from our cage as the rest of the flock flies free into the distance. We now complain about the fate of our future and wonder woefully, *if only I had listened to the wise one*. This wise one resides within each of us!

You have what it takes to capture the world. There is no need to procrastinate anymore. The Creator has blessed you with many spiritual tools, use them wisely to get where you want to go. Choose your friends and build a relationship that is reciprocal in all matters and in your favour.

We may face challenges along the way, but that is part of life's experiences which shape us into who we are today. So, take flight and spread those wings. Embrace everything that the world has to offer. Take that leap of faith that everyone is always talking about. Remain faithful to your cause and you will live to see the dawn. As it rises, so too will your opportunities to make everything right in your world. Like the phoenix, you will rise from the ashes and be reborn while embracing a new way of living. No longer will you struggle to find the answers, for they are right there.

Some have become afraid to stop outside of home in case they are confronted by unfriendly people. You have no need to fear this sort of thinking. Just be aware of your surroundings and use your intuition more. If something does not feel right, don't go there. Your body is a highly sophisticated band of energy and can pick up on angry individuals easily. Take a look at where you're going. The body or intuition will send you warning signals. It's quite fascinating; all you need to do is listen to the God within. We surround you with the loving Christ light.

Nothing is impossible. Human beings seek approval and reassurance that they are doing the right thing. You do not need anyone's approval to undertake or go ahead with what you want in this life. Many are driven by expectations from others. Use your own intuition, for you alone are a force to be reckoned with, and only you can make the best decisions for you. Take responsibility for you.

Listen with your heart and act on your intuition; you know that it is always right.

Jesus

And so, He came to Earth as a babe and three wise men followed the star that would lead them to the master Yeshua, lying in his humble bed.

Nurtured by his Earthly mother and supported by his Earthly father. The story goes that he was born on the twenty-fifth day in December, and we celebrate this day of his birth yearly. The great master is called the Son of God, and throughout his lifetime, so many countries taught and preached the word of God, performing miracles along the way. Yeshua was born to know his destiny and how he would return to the Father.

Yeshua was born a human being and yet performed so many wonderful things that everyone wanted to follow him, and be like him. There is so much reference in the Bible that speaks of human beings having the same attributes as Yeshua.

The Bible verse John 10:30 explains how this could be: 'I and the Father are one'.

This verse is just one of many found in the Bible. So, if we are made in the image of God, and we are more than what we think we are, then we should be able to heal ourselves and be kinder to others around us, having compassion and love for those who have harmed us. This is a very hard thing to do.

Those who are brave enough take up the challenge of enlightenment, and for whatever reason, they do this to take them to the next level of awareness. They find that there must be more to life than the one they are currently living in, and it draws them closer to loving themselves more and finding out who they truly are. We are the children of God; he does not have any expectations of us nor does he punish us, for there is no judgement. We live our lives the best we can and are blinded by material goods that flood our thoughts. Stress plays a major factor in our daily lives. We need to learn to have more faith in ourselves, for in doing so, we have faith in God, who loves us unconditionally.

Scribe: Tell me about Jesus. So much has been written about him.

He was a master, Dear One. The only human to have ever come to his full potential, here to show the human beings that they have the DNA instilled within to do what Christ could do. Born a human being and died a human being, for that was his quest, to bring about love, peace and joy to the world. One man who had done so much, guided by the Father, the Divine Source of pure love and compassion. Many mentors guided him through his journey. He, too, had written parchments that described his union with the Source and how he completed the tasks set before him to become stronger in his faith, and to live and breathe unconditional love.

Dear One, they scribed on wood and dried animal skin, and etchings were also found on stone.

Human beings misinterpreted his love for humanity and changed his words over the course of time. Although the Christ was born to be sacrificed, his teachings became misconstrued as to why he was here. He came to remind human beings to love each other even though they may have a different belief system or religion, faith, culture, skin colour, etc. You, Dear One, are part of one race – the human race.

The Christ came to try to change your way of thinking, but even his own followers got it wrong through the ages. A great example is that which has occurred during his millennia. We do not need to write about those facts because it is well publicised. How they can take the Christ's teachings and turn it into a circus is beyond our belief. The time will come again, and he will walk the Earth again and bring it all back into alignment.

Scribe: Can you please tell me whether the Christ is here already?

Yes, the Christ is back and is here again to bring humanity into balance.

Scribe: Where does he reside and has he been reborn?

He has not been reborn, as he has already been through the process of being a human being. He is indeed a fully grown adult and resides in isolation as such a time, he will reappear to right the wrongs of the Father.

Scribe: What does that mean?

Love and peace shall reign again, the truth will be told, and the darkness will fold. The wrongs of the Father mean giving humanity another chance, and the darkness will not succeed. Without dark, there is no light, and vice versa. Now, there will be a balance of all things.

Scribe: Where is Mary Magdalene buried?

Louvre Museum, Rue de Rivoli, Paris, France. Mary Magdalene came from an affluent family, she was not what they said she was. We could say she was a female version of Jesus; she had the ability to heal the sick. She gave birth to Jesus' children.

Scribe: Did she die of natural causes?

We cannot say for sure, but her immune system had failed her. She may have been poisoned slowly, whether that was intentional or whether she had a weakness from a particular food group, this information is not exact. We do know that she lived for a while longer than expected in those times.

Scribe: Is there more information you would like to share with us regarding Mary Magdalene?

Know that she was a scholar; very bright, clever, generous, loving, kind, and compassionate, a true martyr. Know that she fled persecution just as much as Jesus. Their bloodline still continues to exist to this day. They will not say who they are, for if they do, there will be detrimental consequences. There are many people who would try to extract their

DNA, blood and everything else for sample testing. Human beings will want to change their own molecular DNA structure to align with Jesus' DNA! What human beings don't realise is, Jesus was a human being, albeit a highly evolved and advanced soul.

Jesus developed his skills far beyond and stretched his limits. He tested everything, sat with the masters and developed natural abilities. That is why he was brought to Earth, to experience a human existence. Dear One, what makes you think the master Jesus had only one wife? What if I told you he had more than one wife and many children! What would society and your history books have to say about that? Today, there are many stories pertaining to who Jesus was, none are truly accurate. Truth be told, you all keep guessing.

God is one with all. We must always remain curious, ask questions often and know thyself more.

Journey

When any journey comes to an end it can be sad, but it is also a change to celebrate the completion of a project, a relationship, a job, a holiday or even a goal. The journey may have been the hardest to endure, and yet you managed and learned so much along the way. Well done, you! The ups and downs you must have encountered along the way would have been challenging, but here you are, all done and dusted and ready to take on another adventure and see it to completion. For every milestone you reach there is another to conquer. Be brave, Dear One, you have come so far and done so much in this lifetime. Excellence is an understatement for what you have managed over time. We say again, well done, you! Keep going, you still have much to do and learn. We must never stop learning and doing.

May peace be with you night and day and as you feel it in every way. We wish the light shines bright to show you where to go. May you be happy and free. Live your life the best you can and make sure you look after yourself.

> *"The journey of a thousand miles begins with one step."*
> – Lao Tzu

Judgement

The word itself conjures up all sorts of ideas. How do we judge and why? Predominantly, it is about people who do not fit into 'normal' society. They are the ones who look and live differently, and we have decided they should no longer be allowed to express themselves openly.

Freedom to express oneself is a given right; it is soul-destroying, and above all, the meanest betrayal anyone could put upon a person to question that. Not everyone is judgemental, for they have learned lessons, and the only reason they are not is because they have a loved one in that situation. Whether they are being judged for their disability, mental health, or the colour of their skin, the list is endless. It goes so far as someone not wearing the right clothing, shoes or earrings.

> *"Judge not, that ye be not judged."*
> – Matthew 7:1

Kailash Mansarovar

Scribe: What is the Kailash Mansarovar phenomena from Tibet?

The mountains of the Gods are sacred to the beings that live beneath the waves; intelligent little creatures.

Scribe: They say that they are a collective.

Yes, as you human beings are. You think you work independently but your energy can be felt wherever you walk and sit. These creatures have evolved to transmit very powerful electronic pulses that could ultimately kill a human being.

Why do humans have to invade their space? What business is it to compromise the little beings' space? They are not hostile creatures and yet humans want to test them to see how they respond.

Human beings will always interfere with something that they are unfamiliar with. They want to know how these beings function and what their intentions are while on Earth. The energy these entities possess is part of their survival tactic. They are God's creation – a single-celled proton neuron element. These creatures live beneath the water and give off a high vibration. Whoever visits this place will ultimately feel their presence. Caution is required when entering the water.

We have all been indoctrinated in our own cluster or group of beings. Do you not think they have their own gurus or sentient masters who teach themselves about humans and what they are capable of? We are not separate from other forms. We go from one human existence and experience to another, learn what we need to, and move on. What we continue to look for is something we have already been. Is that to confirm that we have been, for example, an alien on a different voyage? Does it give the human self-satisfaction knowing that they were right in thinking they were that particular being? Hopefully, it helps the human to settle into their current existence once they find what they are looking for, like a piece of the puzzle that fits.

Humans are habitual creatures. They go about their business daily, and then one day, they awaken and realise there is more to this life than what they are currently experiencing. The search begins for their true selves.

Yes, some humans are content to sit their whole life without curiosity and believe that this is all there is. But those brave enough will step forward and embrace whatever they feel they want to experience.

Religion has a big part in duping humans into believing only one reality exists. This is a form of controlling the many, and this has been so for many generations of humans. The belief in one way of thinking has become the downfall of humanity.

When silence breaks, the end is near, the end of frustrating times. Listen to the beat of the Divine pulsing through your body. God of Gods, Lord of Lords, are here to assist you with all there is.

> *Miraculous elements exist on our planet;*
> *learn to respect all that there is.*

Kundalini

This subject was introduced to me by a friend. I had no idea what this was until I experienced it all. The dizziness and uncontrollable shaking while asleep were overwhelming.

Dear One, it is I, Elohim.

Scribe: Welcome Elohim, please tell me about the Kundalini.

You have experienced it all, Dear One. The vibration that has been surging through your temple. All of the physical awakenings in your body, the pain, blockages and equilibrium disorder. The dark night of sorrow is also one of these symptoms related to the activation of the Kundalini.

Scribe: Why does it need to be activated like this?

I can explain that it is like a light switch turned on. The electricity build-up is so strong that the currents are too much for the body, which causes the blockages in the body to build and then explode. The energy is trapped and has nowhere to go, thus causing the person to feel unwell mentally, physically and psychologically until the energy is released. It's about riding through the experience.

The hour has arrived; step forward, you have experienced all that you need to. Congratulations, you have come out of the dark into the light; you rode with it and accepted everything even though you had no idea what your body was going through. The transformation was happening internally.

Scribe: I have heard that some people want to awaken their Kundalini. Is it possible to initiate that?

It is better for the recipient to receive a natural response, for the Kundalini is not something that everyone is prepared for. For some, the release can drive them almost insane if they do not know what is happening, for others it is not so vicious. It is a whole new shift and understanding about the Earth, the Universe and oneself.

Scribe: I find that amazing! I am so happy that I have experienced this and know now that I am on the right track.

The Kundalini mainly activates in those who are seeking spiritual enlightenment as they know that there is something within them that they do not fully understand. Every one of you seeks something you know is missing from your lives; some choose religion to fill that gap. They then move on until such a time as something else resonates.

The mystics have helpers that bend to their every need; they treat them like Gods. That is the way of it. If humans knew they also have the potential, the only presence they would bow to would be the Source that resides in each and every one of them. It is not to be compared to ego. This is not ego, this is merely a fact stating that ye are all the spark of the Divine.

Scribe: From what I've been told, when the Kundalini awakens or is released, it's like a serpent that travels up your spine. Is this true? No one has really fully explained what, where or how it came about. My next question is, who discovered this?

Break down to understand the meaning: KUN-DA-LINI; centre of the spectrum; the awakening of a human at a deeper level. Consciousness, subconsciousness, third eye, soul, spirit, Kundalini, body. We wonder why we are so confused; all have their part to play in the existence of a human being. Understanding half of this is getting closer to awakening.

Scribe: Having to balance everyday life and living is also a challenge. How does one even begin to comprehend the complexity of it all?

When we look at all these elements individually, they themselves are made up of different parts. We can sit and analyse every single component of what has been listed and will come to the same conclusion – that the human being is indeed their own planetary system. Movement and acceleration, modalities of the fundamental grasp of internal combustion, one needs to take care when the Kundalini awakens, for as stated, if it comes in too fast, it could cause the human to burn up. We believe this is called human combustion.

There have been noted instances where this has occurred, although there is no proof that entering the Kundalini stage was the cause. Unfortunately, the only thing is that one would never know until it's too late. So, let's hope the Kundalini occurs in trickles, or bit by bit, as to avoid unfortunate accidents.

Celebrate those humans who can tell the difference in what is talking, your mind or body. Celebrate the one who is able to channel the truth through the portal of the consciousness to meld with the higher self while gathering information from Spirit. Be a collector of compassion and unconditional love with esoteric knowledge. Be a mentor for those who seek the light. Do not fear, all is true and correct, Dear One.

We can split into the different components of ourselves: the higher self, which is who we truly are; our corporeal (having a body); the spirit; and most importantly, the soul. Blessed be those who come through me to know themselves. For to know oneself is to know who I am, the living God. For love pours forth and envelops those who stand beside me. The healers do their work without trying because they are already working in synchronicity with the Source of all creation; the energy discharges and affects all who come in contact within a radius of three metres wide.

You will do this unknowingly; for now, you walk with us and us with you. There is no filter, and it is what it is. Put aside your human thinking and focus on the Source and your daily questions shall be answered.

*When I awaken, I am free from
the burdens that hold me.*

Learning

We are forever learning, whether it be with someone, in a group or individually. Learning is something that connects everyone. When you have people in your life who resonate the same energy, of course you will be attracted to their vibration. We connect on a deeper level as well. Whether it is past life patterns between an individual or in a collective group, you will always have that connection because you are from that same consciousness. We come in together, lifetime after lifetime, to fulfil our grand design. Our collective family is always with us during that time of learning. Once we have completed the journey with that particular group, we are moved on and are placed in another group to learn and experience all that they have to offer.

Recycling of ancient knowledge is all there is. We need to learn how to remember, so we do not repeat the same mistakes we did in previous lifetimes.

Once you learn a new skill, you will always have it, but you have to practice every day to keep up with what you've learned. Learning new concepts helps to develop our cognitive processes as well. The brain functions better when it is challenged to learn new and improved ideas and innovative techniques. Our species is curious by nature, so we need to be stimulated, otherwise our brain fogs and can't function as well as it should. Feed the brain materials that will fascinate it; be in awe of a new concept and be wowed at something you have never seen before. We carry within ourselves so many creative ideas that we don't know how exceptional we really are until we try something new.

It may have come from a past life, and you have brought it back to this lifetime. You, too, have a purpose on the Earth plane; seek it, and you shall find it. Open the doors to all possibilities, refine your search and don't take less when you find what you are looking for. Focus on what you're trying to achieve, and have faith that you will find your calling. Everything around you is your playground and all you can do is play the game. Humanity is where one is born into at this moment, at this time. A fraction of you remains with Spirit, and there you are able to connect with God. So there you are, child of the Universe, and we cannot stress enough that you are more than what you claim to be. Some humans know this already and have embraced their destiny fully. Don't wait any longer, do it and find who you truly are.

Life is a game, and it is supposed to be fun. Let us forever make so much fun and laughter within our lives that joy and happiness will always be with us. Lighten up and try not to be so serious all the time. We are here on Earth for such a short time. Let us celebrate the time we have here. There is no time for bitterness, nastiness or pouting lips. Remember why you came. Take a risk; you only have one life, and it is this one. Look after the one body you have in this lifetime and connect with the land around you. The sacred land of the ancient people that once flourished, pay your respects and be grateful.

The more we speak, the less we know. Listen more and let others speak. You may learn something enlightening.

Lemurian

The beautiful, long-figured beings that walked upon the Earth's surface until today. Slender bodies, peace, loving beings; the beginning of the human race. Seeded by The Creator, who bought them alive with his breath and love. Created to bring harmony to the Earth and to live a peaceful existence. For many millennia, they have moved about, showing humans how to behave, grow crops and look after the resources.

They created and charted the stars, moon and sun. Their technology is working with the crystals of the Earth, reverberating the area, sending loud sound waves underground, activating the crystals, helping to heal the planet. In doing so, helping to heal mankind, bringing them to an awareness.

Dear One, you will remember your life as Lemurian. We will show you in your meditation or in your sleep state. You will be able to walk with them. They are your ancient ancestors. They can help to realign your body system to where it is supposed to be. Fear not, I am with thee.

Scribe: What do they eat?

They have evolved to light beings; they no longer need to ingest plant or animal matter. They are of exuberance, like the rays of sunshine that they are. The light energy mainly comes from the Earth and every living being around them, including fauna and flora. Their job is to explode love and receive love like a beacon. They have chosen to remain on the Earth to nurture those who are choosing the path of enlightenment and for others to come into understanding and awakening to the universal laws.

They dwell in caves and are not seen by man, although some humans have claimed to see them.

Scribe: Why are they so secretive?

Dear One, it is not that they are secretive, it is that humans are curious creatures who want to dissect everything to see how it functions; it is the way of it. One hopes that humans will change and start to accept the way things are without pulling them apart for their scientific studies.

Scribe: Do they manipulate mankind?

We have explained to you before about free will. All humans have this, we cannot change that. Angels may whisper, guides will too; in the end it is up to you.

Scribe: There have been many books written about the Lemurian, are they true?

Can you believe what is written here? Do you understand where your information is coming from?

Scribe: Yes, my higher self.

Some have forged someone else's research, while others are doing what you are doing right now. We are only scratching the surface.

Blessed are those who use their spiritual gifts to uplift and help all in need.

Light beings

The eyes are the windows to the soul. The left eye signifies the past. The reason it twitches is because whatever you saw back then is starting to be let go of, for it no longer serves you at this time. See it for what it is and release. Thank and acknowledge that was then, this is now. Forgiveness from past trauma, let go of it.

Scribe: I am grateful to have gone one more step ahead in my walk with Spirit. Thank you, all celestial beings, for your love and support always. To be initiated into the celestial realm is beyond overwhelming.

Dear One, each and every one of you have been touched with our healing presence. Wherever you go, whatever you do, we are with you. Human beings will experience our healing through you, for we reside with you, and we resonate at a very high level of vibration. That is why you will never feel your energy deplete, as there is no energy exchange; let us be clear about that. We help you to become a better version of yourself, if you want to accept.

Scribe: In my dream state, I was initiated by the Source into the realms of light beings; this is my account of what occurred as I slept. I was taken to the celestial realm; I kneeled on one knee (like the thinking man) in front of the almighty Source and was anointed with oil. I felt an overwhelming unconditional bright love and light emanating within me and around me, where I became initiated into the celestial realm. I felt honoured as they telepathically thanked me for helping someone through a Reiki healing session.

What I experienced was a test for me to hold myself together because what I witnessed was not of God while I was healing. The celestial beings helped me to calm, and I felt well and truly protected as I was healing. I will not go into too much detail as it was private and confidential. Much of the healing I do is. As I recited, 'The Lord is my shepherd', Psalm 23,

I was grateful that I had the support of my helper with me, as we are on the same wavelength.

The flood gates have now opened it is grand to know that everything is well and you, Dear One, are taken good care of. Be at peace, always at peace. Be patient, happy; no need to be sad. Forgive and know that the past is the past. The lessons have all been and gone, growth for you now is top priority; growth in your walk with us. Dear One, I am here and so proud of your transition to the higher realms. We celebrate your progress and delight in what is to come.

I never knew the sun would shine again.
I never knew someone like you.
Thank you for bringing the
light back to my door.
I am truly thankful and grateful forever more.

Light codes

Scribe: What are light codes?

Think of the way a body is made up, the way it functions or why it functions at all. You could say that each individual human being is their own planet. What happens in the core of your bodies is the same as what happens within the Earth's core; the indigenous peoples all know this. Observe a tree and the way it branches out; they are the lungs of the Earth. Take a good look and you will see the root system is the placenta. The nutrients are fed through the root systems, similar to a baby in the womb. We are all connected. We are born. We die. The Earth is the same and like all human beings, if we do not take care of ourselves, we are in trouble. Yes! We can have those band-aid fixes that are temporary, but in the end, we succumb to our own deeds.

The light codes are the sparks of life that give us the direction of where to work. They are similar to a vehicle light system; one turns green, another amber, and finally, red for stop. Light codes have been sent to you via higher masters, or beings, to help with your elevation. The intention is to awaken your vibration to help heal the planet.

We cannot express ourselves more about humans being a collective, although we understand that humans are curious beings and ask too many questions instead of getting the job done. Why not ask the question later, after the job is done?

Ego for the human is a huge challenge, especially when there is work to be done, but the harvesting keeps being put on the back burner. We sit here and are in awe of this species that has the answer and yet doesn't. The potential that humans have is beyond their own capabilities, knowing that if they play their cards right no one on this Earth should be sick, hungry, abused, raped, and the list goes on. You humans fear too much. The more you fear, the stronger the negative forces dance. This is what holds you back.

God has no judgement on where or what your choices are. We cannot interfere. Light codes are sent through the physical body via the pituitary gland, and those light codes signal to the body to resonate pure love and energy to all those who are willing to change by not forgetting the internal body.

I wish for you abundance, prosperity, kindness, compassion, and most of all, unconditional love.

Love

One of the biggest healing practices that everyone has access to is love. Anyone can conquer anything with the power of loving thoughts. We can love ourselves; we can love each other and our pets; we can also love what we do. Unconditional love is where there are no expectations put on anyone. Love is a strange word; no one can really describe it, even though we can feel it and see it in action.

When you read something that touches your heart or see something out in the environment, perhaps you hear music that was related to a time when you were in love, with your senses firing on all cylinders, igniting a spark within your body. How do we even define what love is? The love of the Divine Source to find peace with oneself and wholly love who you are. You have found the one true love of your life, and that is God within. The love of one's life can also relate to someone who is your soul mate. The one you want to spend the rest of your life with.

Finding and connecting with the higher self is also an experience of pure bliss and love. For every truth comes from this place of authenticity. The breath of life. The all-encompassing white light of God's embrace; this is love. For God so loved the world He gave his only son, so he that believes in Him shall have everlasting life not just in this lifetime, but beyond the veil.

Precious you are, indeed, you are all God's creation. He has sent you here to experience the world and to know that you can rely on Him when things get a little tough. We are all here for a reason and a purpose. Love can be a gesture of goodwill and is felt throughout your whole body. When you do things for others, the feeling is so great; it's like a fulfilment. When you look outside, cast your eyes at the miracles of life, and you will fall in love with the trees and the plants, the sky, and the moon. It always amazes me, God's gift to humanity.

When love finds you, embrace it and keep it. This is your ace card and it trumps all other cards; it even stands above the queen. When you look in the mirror and don't like what you see, pull out your trump card. Yes, your *love* card. This is who you are. You are God's child, the love of His life, created in His image. So, remember when you are down, take a look at your love card and read it out aloud.

Feel it in your heart and hold it in your soul, for everyone looks for love and thinks it's nowhere to be found. So now that you know that love is all around you, be at peace with yourself and know God loves you and always will. There is no judgement, and time heals all, so never feel ashamed to let your guard down. Life is full of wonder; go out there and experience it all. Take your love card with you to remind you. One day, you may want to hand it to someone else who needs it so they, too, can remember who they are.

I come to thee with comfort, love and readjustment. Feel my love, know my love. We have travelled the cosmos together many lifetimes over energy intertwined; we both bring hope, care and love to all humanity. Dear beloved, we rode together through time and space searching for peace on different planets, bringing with us our all-compassionate existence. My love for you does not exist on Earth; it belongs to the cosmos of infinity. We are love, we give love, and we walk love. We are not separate from it. Much work to do, many souls to reach. The time for the collective awakening to occur.

Love is like medicine. Taken every day, it can cure anything.

Luck

Luck has nothing to do with anything; we decide for ourselves what we want in life. There are miracles that occur in our lives and synchronicity also becomes apparent. So, does that mean you wait until miracles or synchronicity happen in order to feel fulfilled? You cannot wait for any of these to come along, you must continue your life and make the best of any situation. When you are on the right path, miracles will appear, whether you are aware of them is another story.

I believe we are already destined somehow. During this lifetime, we go through trials and tribulations that bring us to where we are meant to be. The puzzle pieces fit together perfectly, and there is awareness when you realise what you have gone through has led to where you are today. I have personally witnessed weird and wonderful happenings, and nothing surprises me anymore. If you listen closely enough, you will be led to where you are supposed to be.

Today, I accept the world as it is.

Manifest

I have given you everything that life can provide, and you can manifest anything you want. There is no need to rely on anyone but yourself. Powerful are those who walk in the light and take from it the unconditional love of the Divine. We enter this realm all naked and lost, and we have parents who take care of our needs until we can do it ourselves. We grow from a society that dictates everything to us, and we watch all sorts of weird and wonderful movies for entertainment; we even try to mimic some of them and get ideas. There is nothing wrong with that, but you all have your own perfect reality, and you can connect to anything you want. So don't be like the majority; find your own pathway and make sure it's clear before you step onto the right track.

You all have tools, so use them wisely, and you will enjoy your lifetime in your own perfect way. We love you eternally.

> *"If you love life, life will love you back."*
> – Arthur Rubinstein

Masters

While there have undoubtedly been many advanced beings that have progressed humanity forward in leaps and bounds, we all are masters within ourselves.

Scribe: Leonardo da Vinci, the famous painter, inventor, scientist and overall the most curious human being that ever walked the Earth, not one day of his life was wasted doing absolutely nothing. From a very young age, he studied plants and insects by observing them and their life patterns. The paintings and sketches he produced were captivating and so real; he must have had all the beings and masters working with him and alongside him.

Leonardo da Vinci was a master unto himself – an advanced soul. He came to Earth to share his knowledge and leave behind a legacy so others may follow in his footsteps. Masters will come back to Earth every so often when they are called upon to enlighten a lost generation that forgets how history was and hopefully not repeat the bad things that happened. As for famous artists, their gift to the world was the insight into beauty on canvas and all the creativity that goes with it. Not many have been reborn yet who come close to the magnificence of the Renaissance period. Time has moved on, and so has modern creativity and art.

Scribe: It would be a miracle to own one of his pieces or to even sketch like he does.

Dear One, you are an artist in your own right. You are the writer, although you may not think so; the words you have written for us are amazing already. A year has passed, and already, you have been challenged beyond your capacity. You have been challenged to expand your way of receiving our information and formulating and even interpreting our delivery. When the masters come back and are reborn to the Earth, they pick up the new technology and expand its value to enhance the human race and preserve the environment. Unfortunately, greed still reigns in many human beings in power. The only way new technology can be taught truthfully is to take the greedy capitalists off their mark and replace them with those who are not ego-driven. Heads of state need to get together and not be afraid of what is to come.

> *Be who you were born to be,*
> *the mighty – I am.*

Meaning of life

Scribe: What is the meaning of life?

Life is the beginning of anything that is living. A human being is created from the time of conception. What about the mighty oak tree that started as a seedling? This is life, but living is something else.

In order to live life, one must figure out first how you would like to live life, or perhaps what lessons you want to learn and how you're going to learn them.

I ask now for the Golden light to be sent to enable a wonderful gift of living and breathing. All is well. The Lord Divine is in your protective love and grace.

Scribe: What does that mean?

Remember who and what you are, the sacred entity of the Divine. Sacred means light to the touch and powerful of energy. Be very gentle, as you would when you touch a feather; feel the sacredness of your being.

This, my beloved Dear One, is what and who you are. So, my message to you is to be gentle like the feather. Be delicate to yourself. Treat yourself as you would your best friend. Just be who you truly are; the soft nature of Jesus, who walked Earth as a human. The same DNA resides in you. All are the same and unique at the same time. Create love and be loved; that is all we ask of you all.

Everyone on this planet has their own interpretation of life and what it means to them, and that is a good thing because it means you are exercising your rights as a human being and not giving into what is termed conditioning. What you perceive in this lifetime is what life means to you. Anything is open for discussion and interpretation. We all see and hear things in a different way. It is up to us to distinguish where any of it belongs. Never let anyone tell you that your interpretation is wrong. There are too many theorists out there who claim to have all the answers through studying a particular subject and coming up with their own conclusions.

Humans are born, and they die; what happens in between is up to you to create. Have fun with your life. You know that there is only one go while you're here. Why not make it interesting? Find ways to let things happen for you. Great things build character; don't be afraid to step out and step forth. We are not limited by any means, and we encourage you to feel alive and breathe deeply. Be a positive leader for those who are stuck in their misery. Life is not meant to be like that. Reprogram your mind, and please do not be afraid to express yourself fully. Don't worry about who is watching; let them watch; maybe something will rub off on them, too. At least when you pass you can say to yourself, *Yes! I did it!* Be at peace with yourself and love yourself more. We encourage you always and will be by your side. We are The Collective, the galactic force sent by The Creator to keep and inspire you all!

> *In front of you lies an amazing journey; follow your life path.*

Meditative consciousness

Abundance rises up to meet you. Samadhi is a condition of consciousness where you lose your own and merge with God, uniting with the consciousness of The Creator. You think not with your own mind, nor with the feelings of the flesh. The higher self merges with God and you feel the bliss and know this only comes from The Creator.

You are then in touch with all wisdom and all truth, and you feel and know everything there is to know. This condition is a gift from God that you earn when you are ready for it. You will never be the same again, for you can never forget or be separate from the feeling of bliss and great peace. You will only want God and have an overwhelming desire to seek Him more and more. Seek ye first the kingdom of God, and all these things will be given unto you.

Knock and the door will open unto you, and a new day dawns. Dreams come true, and the spark has been lit. Follow those dreams, and you can become anything you want. Do not let fear get in the way, for ego will try to strike at you if you allow such a thing. Create wonderful people around you for yourself, ones who will always be positive, loving and kind.

Meditation brings peace to the mind as it quietens itself. It's time for reflection and no thought at all.

Just to be in silence without doing is an achievement in itself. Still the chatter and quiet the mind.

Memories

Memories are what we have that linger inside of us, they are of childhood dreams, and those that we have left behind. The memories of loved ones gone, and of holidays of wind, surf and beach parties with barbeques galore; the beautiful sunrise and sunsets; your first true love and more. The first-born child and the sleepless nights have now become a blur, the kids have all grown up and the grandchildren have arrived. There are more memories to share with them, memories from your past. Some you want to forget, and others you hope will remain with you forever, like the face of your mother and father, the wonderful life you had as a child, the traditional food, and Christmas that have never stood the test of time. Everything has changed now, and you are the grandparent. As a child, you thought you would never see grey hair on your head. You soon share your stories with your children and grandchildren the way your parents shared theirs.

Past life memories and dreams of far-off exotic continents that you wish to visit one day. Past life memories of a time when you may have lived there, for the culture seems so familiar to you and resonates with you on a grand scale. We have lived so many thousands of lifetimes, and it is no wonder we are confused when the life we now live becomes tangled with the past. Memories are all we have of everything we've done. Some people have amazing memories, while others care not to remember because the past is so hurtful.

Some have advanced souls, and their memories are like those of computers or calculators. I am sure they have bought that from a previous lifetime beyond the galaxy. Now, I am a writer and have had, I'm sure, a past life remembrance. It makes sense because prior to me writing with Spirit, I had never had this type of knowledge. I am not an articulate person at all, but the words walk across the page, and I know exactly where each word fits. If this is a memory, then wow, it's a great memory.

"I think, therefore I am."
– René Descartes

Mind

When you look through the eyes of the body you wear, what do you see? The outside world looking back at me, which some find a scary place to be. We have set routines every day just to survive the mundane. We live with: eat, sleep, work and repeat. The torment inside the mind is restless, like a separate entity that rules the body and the consciousness within. They fight to maintain balance and some people lose the battle. They give up because their minds are too strong, and they end up taking over. Balance in one's life seems to be the answer to all life's battles. We are tortured by the unwillingness to participate in our life. We make excuses and blame others for our disposition or our seemingly dysfunctional lives. Some are medicated to bring them back into balance, others are put away in places that are supposed to help them with their mental illness.

We fail as a society to help each other to understand what others may be lacking in their lives. Functionality is all one strives for within one's life, and continuously asks the mind to stop chatting so much. That is what anyone asks for, peace and stability and a decent, manageable type of living and knowing themselves well enough to know what the body is trying to say.

If we become more in tune and listen to the needs of our body, the body will reciprocate and deliver exactly what it wants and needs. Nurture and love your body and yourself because you only have one chance in this lifetime to make something of yourself. It is not material things, it is a lifetime of wisdom, knowledge and understanding. Helping others to achieve their goals is also a great purpose, and nothing is more rewarding than helping your fellow man. It is wonderful to watch others bloom in their totality and to let you know they finally get life. It is very satisfying to know you have made a difference wherever you go.

Many lives we have lived, balance is the key.

Mindfulness

You see the word mindfulness often in esoteric books, magazines and articles and it has filtered through to the mainstream in a big way. They always say things like meditation is about being mindful. Practising mindfulness involves breathing methodologies and techniques guided by imagery and other practices to relax the body and mind, helping to reduce stress.

Scribe: Focusing on the food you are consuming is also mindfulness. You can also be mindful about what you say to others and the way you conduct yourself. Mindfulness also extends to maintaining a moment-by-moment awareness of your thoughts, feelings, bodily sensations and surroundings through different lenses. In other words, living in the present. Mindfulness brings us to the present moment. Its roots were introduced by Buddhist monks it is a translation of sati, *a word in the Pali language of ancient India that means 'awareness.' At the end of the day, be mindful about what you say, think and do, what you put into your mouth and also what comes out of it. For what comes around goes around.*

*The Universe is alive and listening
and responding to your request.*

Miracles

Miracles happen; this is called Divine intervention and synchronicity at its finest. When we doubt ourselves, we are giving way to negative thoughts. We are only human, and we possess the most incredible walking machine that has been given to us. The complex machine is the human body, mind, and soul encased in such a miraculous form. How we treat it is our own choice. There is no manual on how one treats or mistreats their body, but society and environmental changes all have an influence on how you will live your life. You can always change your lifestyle.

A miracle occurs when you realise you do not have to be who society dictates you to be. Explore the real you, the authentic person you were born to be and express yourself freely. There is a lot going on right now, and it's all good. It means there is a new generation of children being born who are not going to tolerate injustice. We are slowly evolving, and humanity will no longer be the way we see it now. Change is always good; it gives us opportunities to recreate ourselves.

> *"There are only two ways to live your life. One is as though nothing is a miracle. The other is as though everything is a miracle."*
> – Albert Einstein

Mother Earth (Gaia)

Mother Earth can never be owned. Humans think they have the right to her land, water and air; they are wrong in so many ways.

Treat her with respect as all ancient cultures do and she will flourish again and give you what you need, be kind, be honest, be courteous to her, love her eternally as you have love for your family. As you abide by these rules, bountiful fruits will be given to those who adhere. We are all visitors and we must remember it is so.

The beat and rhythm of life go on; listen to the sound of Mother Earth heaving instead of breathing, her lungs congested with so much pollution she too has to elevate herself to accommodate the changes brought about by mankind.

Is it fair to say we are not doing enough to help her? She is trying to change to accommodate human beings. Why would she do that? Because she needs you as much as you need her. Elevated humanoids activate her gridlines and the energy force; therefore Mother Earth is also protected by them. The more human beings become aware, the faster she will heal. Think of how you can send healing to Mother Earth, and so it shall be.

We pollute the air and the waterways, and we never learn that water is more priceless than gold. We live in a throwaway society, and our rubbish becomes remnants of our carelessness. We throw away so many recyclable materials and objects that can be reused, and we throw away food, and yet there are thousands starving. What is wrong with society? We are greedy, nonsensical beings. We live in a rubbish tip that remains with us for thousands of years. Time is not on our side, and we have nothing going on for us. I do not like to be negative, but the stuff we are going through is horrendous to the planet and to ourselves. Let's clean up our act and do something before it's too late. Time is ticking like a bomb.

Flowers bloom whenever you're around. They sense your beautiful energy and sounds.

Music

How is it that a song is played, and immediately we are transported to a time we had initially heard it? They say that if you hear a particular song over and over again, it is a memory, or something you need to learn. Listen to the lyrics of the song; all songs have been sent from the Divine Universe for everyone to grasp meaning. The Universe has directed the lyrics and melodies to tell you something.

So the next time you continuously play a song, ask yourself, "What is the Universe trying to say to me?" I'm sure it will answer all your bottled-up questions that you may have forgotten. Remember there are times we feel lost and perhaps a little lonely. We listen to familiar sounds or music to cheer us up or to mend a broken heart. Don't take life or your loved ones for granted because they are the ones who love you unconditionally and will stand by you even when a storm brews and you have no control.

Music is a gift given to the world, the sound that travels to the soul, the vibration that uplifts the individual and sends messages to the whole being, igniting passion, enlightenment and creativity. Channelled energy is now surging through the Universe. The Angels sing with their choir of songs, trumpets sound and the bells jingle; the flute plays its heavenly tunes and the whole world is lit up with Angelic music.

The ears are happy, and the body too, they are blissfully unaware that everything is synchronising and stirring within. We are all in a happy place when we are transported to a time where we met our first true love or lost a loved one, the music takes us back to the remembrance of those times. Music and singing bring with them a celebration and so much joy that we sing and dance. We love and uplift ourselves in the most eloquent ways. Classical music, rock 'n' roll, hip hop, reggae, the blues – no matter what your choice of music, they all bring us euphoria.

The heavenly choir of Angels sing with you.

New beginnings

Every person goes through the stage of new beginnings. Throughout one's lifetime, challenges will arise when one door closes and another opens. It's a good thing because it tests your ability to learn more and experience new possibilities. The new beginning of a life, a new home, a job, or even the end of a job means you have moved on to find another adventure in life. How exciting is that? It increases the hormone serotonin, encouraging creativity and thought-provoking ideas. Changing jobs or doing something you have never done before, life becomes so exciting and good for the soul. Experience all you can while you are able to. You will never know when life changes, and thoughts of *I should have/would have* come to mind. Enjoy your life, Dear One, and remember you are here for that reason. Live, love and feel alive. We are only a breath away from not being here! Be at peace and love what you do!

New energy and the consciousness uplifting into ascension the shift into higher frequencies and vibrations are entering the atmosphere at this very moment, altering the DNA within the human being and filtering the disease that has been rampant within our society. People are exiting very quickly; some are returning to Earth as newborns to complete their mission as light workers. New relationships are developing, and leaving behind the old beliefs that no longer serve us have now shifted. Paradigms begin to move and change over time. We live in a society that is evolving, however it seems to remain custom built for the rich to get richer and the poor to remain where they are. People who are smart enough to play the game that society has to offer will not be tied to banks and mortgages. The big guys always win, while the small ones still run on the treadmill day after day. It is not a bad thing; it is the way it is, and it is an honest way to make a living. That is why The Creator gave you a body. We have been moving into another dimension since 2003.

You have become a collector of lifetimes on this planet and beyond with the creation of new beginnings each time.

Nourishment

The human consciousness, the higher innate self, is the second brain. You have a conceptual and quantum, smart body. This shared intelligence means you always know what is happening in your body. Learn to recognise intuitive thoughts, talk to your cells, and visualise picking up the phone to listen to your insides. Speak on the phone, "Dear cells, are you listening?" Tell them what you want them to do.

You can slow down the ageing process by speaking to your own body and asking what diet will help you to become more enlightened. Innately your body knows the right food, previously eaten from the past lifetimes you lived. Listen to your instinct and feel for the chills that will come when choosing the right foods. The Arkash knows better, and eats like a Lemurian: soups, salads, and vegetables – less meat or no meat.

Sweetness brings the flowers that bloom. The songs of the birds and nature are alive. Focus on the truth, and the love that surrounds you.

Scribe: Elohim, please show me the opening of a new flower about to burst free, the lotus flower which brings great fortune, purity and above all the sharing of love.

Dearest One, your life on Earth will be so much simpler and easier to maintain once you have mastered the art of healthier alternatives to cooking practices. Herbal teas, beautiful soups, wholesome and beautiful energy bars, or energy balls. There is so much information out there and recipes to help balance your energy by eating properly.

Eating crappy food is not to be restricted. There are too many rules. If it doesn't feel good, don't do it. It will soon shift. The food you eat will not change your ability to ascend. We have a choice in believing what we want. Food is food depending on what your vibratory rate is at. Pay attention to your own beliefs; scientific proof is not always right. Know the difference between your body's vibrating cravings and emotional cravings. This is serving you by increasing the vibration rate. Accept your human self, take off the shackles of diet and food and trust what you are moving towards.

Scribe: Let the healing of my body commence.

Dear One, this is your path to follow. Be brave, be strong, and know that perfect health is your desired outcome; the benefit of a healthy body becomes a healthier you. Clarity of thought, connection with us, clearer walking and talking with confidence, love, and compassion, knowing who you truly are without doubt.

Your desire for sweets will soon dissipate into the nothingness from where it began. Your love for fruit and vegetables will resurface and your desire to seek these foods will become normalised as the old ways become less and less common. Before you know it, these will be the only food your body will be able to assimilate and digest. Everything else will become toxic.

My body is a living temple.

Numerology

Numbers, the universal voice through the ages. Vibrations, frequencies are all calculated by numbers. The grid lines on the Earth make up lots of light shows, so when human beings walk upon the Earth the gridlines light up very much like a shoe print, showing where the frequency or energy is coming from. Different numbers affect what we do in everyday living. It is there in our birth date, and of course, the date we cease on Earth. All the stars are charted in this manner.

Numbers represent the sun, moon and stars, the infinite Universe. Time lapses that create ripple effects count how many ripples make up how many lifetimes you've lived. Timing is right with numbers. Your age determines what lifetime you have come into. Create for yourself another way of living.

Scribe: I see so much balance and harmony in numbers. Perhaps the love for numbers will reappear and I will no longer be afraid to put two and two together. Why are numbers such a hard thing to grasp? They cause me a lot of anxiety and yet I understand that numbers are the galactic language that all beings must know and thrive from.

Dear One, *you* are the universal language. Numbers do not come quickly to you because you have no use for them. Suppose numbers do not come naturally to a human being. It does not mean anything. It only means your capacity to engage in what we call speech of numbers is not your strength; your talent lies elsewhere. We cannot all be the same. We can't all be accountants and crunch the numbers. We will guide you in whatever way we can.

We understand what you are thinking about, Dear One. Do not let what is happening destroy your quest for what you want. Let it be. All things will fall into place the way it ought to be, for God's timing is perfect. There is no need to think about the future and what it holds, for the future changes day by day. Know this, Dear One, your life is already mapped out.

Scribe: What do numbers mean cosmically?

It means alignment and balance not only of energies but also within oneself. This message will be to drop the unnecessary rubbish that people carry day after day. Human beings see it for what it really is. The body gets used to the same pain and adopts the pain, and then it becomes part of their life. So too is the mental anguish that you decide to own because it has been so ingrained within you for you have forgotten what it is like to *not* hold any of this.

Do not create barriers that prevent you from being who you truly are; a wonderfully beautiful soul living a life in a body which can be hurt emotionally and physically. Don't carry the weight of the world upon our shoulders it is worthless to you. Create for yourself the most magical existence you can find; draw it from deep within yourself. There reside the most stunning lifetimes you will create for yourself, leaving behind the lower vibration negative connection such as fear, hatred, and jealousy, which cripple human beings. Stand up for what is rightfully yours.

Scribe: Looking at the number two also brings about balance for me. The right to be heard having fun and having your kind of fun. When I look at the number, it gives me some kind of relief and security, bringing about changes in lifestyle and thinking.

As we expressed before, it is about a new way of doing things – completing tasks that were half finished, having the determination to live life to the fullest. Make recommendations for resources that help complete your mission while on this planet. Whether it is finding others that you are able to relate to or teachers that will be able to keep you on the right track with encouragement and understanding, it will make you accountable for what you are currently doing. All while working with Spirit.

Healing and visualising the atoms of the person's body vibrating in perfect order. Sending healing intentions to each other, 'Where two or more are gathered together in my name, there I am in the midst of them,' Matthew, 18:20.

Scribe: I send healing out into the world, to Mother Earth and the grid. Although we cannot see it, doesn't mean it's not there. We can't see air, but we know it exists otherwise we can't breathe. Birds can fly through the air and they can feel it beneath their wings. Energy is the same; we can't see it, but we feel it in our bodies. When someone is not nice or vice versa, we can sense the energy.

Symbols are found everywhere we look. They are the human beings' secret codes. In society, they represent numerous organisations, cult status and physiological imprint in one's brain and psyche. There are millions around, and humankind has been using them for centuries to manipulate the minds of the human race. They play to extract more money and to get and recruit those who are vulnerable, especially those looking for a place to fit in.

Human beings are, by right, a species of collective thinkers and gravitate towards co-habitation. When they are on their own, their lives become difficult. Although some people live as a recluse by choice, life would become meaningful for all the lonely people out there if they were simply to connect with the people around them.

> *Walk with me, and together, we will learn to shift the barriers that come between us.*

Old soul

Hello old soul. The soul lives on and only the body returns to the Earth to die. We are also on Earth to remember the many journeys that we lived throughout many lifetimes; our relationships with people, places and connections to the Earth are very important for our survival. As an old soul, you come back to Earth to remember why you were sent back. Sometimes, it is to uplift others and to awaken into their own past remembrance. We are all on a pathway to discover our actions while on Earth creating our present situations, so the best thing that you can do for yourself is to make life pleasant and easy. What do you think is the reason you have chosen to reincarnate?

Wherever you go, life is to be loved and nurtured thoroughly. We are here on Earth but briefly. Make the most out of the time you have left, for before you know it, age has caught up with you, and memories tend to fade. Old Soul you are a leader, and you need to interact more with people and accept that you have to help others find us. Be an instrument of The Creator's love.

So, what is the meaning of living, old soul?

Parallel Universe

In letting go of the past it will no longer affect your future. We live a very parallel existence. What happens now also affects both past and future, so make sure, Dear One, that you have made peace with your past so that it does not influence the future negatively.

Scribe: Can you explain a little bit further, please?

We seek the past when the now is affecting our life progress.

Scribe: Do you think current issues may have come from your past?

What if I told you that it could be possible that you may have created the issue at this present time.

Scribe: I have read many books about past regression curing someone with a health problem.

The mind is a very powerful tool on its own; it can either build or destroy someone. You see, your body is not only a temple but also a very complex machine. What makes you think that it is not possible to recreate the same issue today? Your body has a memory, is it not so? The memory also remembers your past life; therefore, recreating symptoms far more difficult than the last.

Scribe: Would it make sense to say you would have increased the volume of whatever an issue it had and brought it forward to this lifetime?

Dear One, I am not saying that seeking past lives is a bad thing, what I am saying is that it is not necessary. Your energy is best used for the *now*.

Scribe: Where do I start with the now issue? It does not seem to be progressing and nothing seems to be happening?

Remember, it takes time even to acknowledge the issue or identify how it is affecting your life.

Scribe: In what way?

Does it cause you sleepless nights?

Does it interfere with everyday living?

Does the issue prevent you from moving forward in life?

Is it causing sickness deeply?

Is it causing mental instability?

Find the issue, acknowledge the issue, find the cause, acknowledge the cause. When these two things are established, slowly, they can be moved through.

The biggest part of this is that. We made a contract with the Divine to learn all we could about our particular issue. How we manage and deal with it is the overall experience. Ride through it, Dear One; it is like a wave. Sometimes it's mighty, and other times very calm. Life is not supposed to be so complicated. Dear One, ask us. We will help and nurture you. We love you eternally.

Scribe: Why is my body moving in and out of itself? Sometimes, it feels like I am projecting another self forward. What is this, or what does it mean?

Dear One, the body is adjusting to the frequencies that are vibrating through you; allow this to happen naturally. Allow the body to rest as it recovers and allow the body to process the food properly and eliminate everything else. The mind will love you for it, and so will your body and soul.

> *"To create one's own world takes courage."*
> – Georgia O'Keeffe

Partnerships

Who are you in partnership with? Who would you *like* to be in a partnership with? What does partnership mean to you? There are so many partnerships we encounter in life; business, exercise buddies, friendships, lovers, you name it. We partner ourselves up with whoever will have us or whoever we are compatible with. Be careful; you may lose your identity or individuality. Partnerships tend to meld or mirror each other after a while because you are constantly agreeing with each other.

In some instances, this is unhealthy. Often, the reason you got together in the first place was your differences and not your similarities. However, whatever is needed at the time, we are not here to judge; we are here to speak about the above. Take your time in choosing your partnerships.

What do you hope to receive from each other? You both need to benefit from the joining of two minds. Creativity and thinking with clarity and honesty, bringing to the table fresh ideas and living a blissful and stress-free life for both parties! Peace be with you!

> *Don't forget to take time for yourself;*
> *everyone deserves a me day.*

Patterns

Scribe: The world is magical. Everywhere you look, people are going about their business with repetitive patterns occurring. Every day seems the same as yesterday. Why is that?

Dear One, human beings live in a loop of existence. You think you are different from the person next door; you are not. Every human being has the same ambition to live a life as perfectly as they possibly can, one of peace, one of harmony and, above all, one of love. To be accepted no matter where they live and how they live. This is all a human being desires in their lifetime here on Earth.

You all come here, my dearest, with no clue or remembrance. You struggle with the contract you signed before you left your true home. For each of you, it is different and yet the same. There are clusters of human beings experiencing the same ways of life. You became like magnets, attracting the same thing. Change the frequency, and the attraction also changes. Groups of human beings all living the same experience.

Very few are different or move to the beat of their own drum. However, they also come in or onto the Earth the same way – as a blind human being – and awoke with knowing the spirit therein. Some are born with special abilities, such as autism and other afflictions that may impede their growth. They are called God's blessings and pure souls, for they carry with them the Divine Source of the Lord at its highest vibration.

We live our lives to please others, only to find we have robbed ourselves of what could have been.

Peace

May peace be with you night and day. May the light of the Lord show you the way. May the sound of His voice ring soft and clear. Be blessed, my dear!

It is with much love and respect for others that brings us to find peace within ourselves. We are but a timeless piece of the puzzle within the Universe; we struggle on Earth to find our calling. We wonder, *is there more to life than raising a family and working nine to five on a daily basis?* One seeks to find the answer to these questions, and more. Sometimes, it takes us a full lifetime. Human beings search and seek until something resonates with them, while others walk the whole length of the world to sit with Sharman and ancient medicine doctors to experience the whole ritual of being between two worlds. My Dear One, it is not found outside of you; it resides within. We are made in the image of the Father; therefore, we have his DNA. Jesus the son became the Messiah who had all of God's attributes – you do too; you just don't know it. Awaken, Dear One.

When we walk in love, all else follows. There will be no pain, no heartache, nor sorrow. Confidence, benevolence and eternal gratefulness will remain. May peace reign with you always.

Perfection

Perfection, what does that mean? The word itself means striving to complete something until it is exact, or to your specifications. A perfectionist is someone with high standards, not only of themselves but of others around them. They are the vain people who love to be around others like themselves. They seem to be flawless; there is no judgement; it is the way they perceive the world and their expectations of everyone else that should reflect the way they feel. Family life should be perfect, their job with fancy high-ranking officials as their perfect little friends, along with celebrities. We are not saying that all these people are perfectionists; we are trying to explain that they will not want to know you if you are not a 'somebody'.

It must be difficult to maintain such a façade and remain at the top of your game even as you grow older. Good for them who look after their appearance and health to look that good, here is hoping they have enjoyed themselves, freedom to express oneself is wonderful.

Graciously, I say unto you that you were made perfect in every way. Remember why you have been sent to Earth. Know your purpose and your purpose will work for you because it is as natural as taking water to drink when you are thirsty. It is what makes you happy in life. You will know when you have found your purpose because it makes your soul come alive and sing. You fall in love with what you do, and all else comes second. Although I think it is always a good thing to be totally balanced in all things and try to restrict yourself from going overboard; otherwise, there is burnout.

Perfection comes with repetition. The more we repeat something, the better we will become. A wood carver will get better over time as he perfects his craftsmanship. A Shaolin monk will perfect kung fu over many years and yet may never be a master. Every day, for twenty-four hours, he will train, and with repetition, he will keep going and never lose focus. Anything you need in life, you must learn how to focus and remain there. Learning too many things at once fragments what you are trying to achieve for yourself. You may be multi-talented, but only one main focus is required. All your energy must remain on one object at a time in order to maintain a stoic stance in all things you do. You are more likely to finish a project if you are fully focused. Scattered thinking brings scattered dreams that start and never seem to finish. Try not to leave too many things incomplete.

It is words of encouragement that we send you right now; the world is your oyster. Love who you are and love what you do. Try and try again. The famous sculptors and painters didn't get it right the first time, but they persevered, never giving up. Now, their paintings and sculptures have been around for hundreds of years, bringing joy to all who are lucky enough to lay their eyes on the original. We must never give up our passion, for it is what we were born to do and share with the world. There have also been some great inventions created that have helped humanity immensely. We are put in a position to unfold our creativity and ideas and to bring them about so others may enjoy them. We share our ideas, too; that is what humans do, and some may even improve on those ideas.

Remember you were born a human being. You must remember to take care of your human form. Love and protect it from diseases and viruses. So gracious also means that one should be courteous, kind and pleasant toward all people regardless. You are one of God's precious children, made in His image, defined by His nature.

May you walk in love and always be who you are. Do not change for anybody.

Pictures

Pictures and photographs capture our imagination and great emotions from the past. Photographs of loved ones, both past and present, line our walls; they bring us comfort every time we look at them. We are in awe as we see our ancestors staring back at us. We notice the same features in them that we have. We comment on how well-groomed they were back then and how very proud they were. The strong presence of them remains with us. Thank your ancestors for creating a pathway of discovery for you.

We also hang up scenic photographs and paintings on our walls to remind us of the outside world and perhaps places that we have visited or wish to visit in the future. We look in amazement at the picturesque and beautiful landscapes provided by nature herself and are amazed at how wonderfully beautiful life is. Famous painters have given us a gift – their masterpieces of an era that has now disappeared; Leonardo Da Vinci, Michelangelo and Claude Monet, just to name a few. Hours of focused, channelled energy created for all to enjoy. The *Mona Lisa* is said to have been painted in 1503; most people speculate about who she was. Who would have thought that such a painting would fetch millions?

Human beings are so messed up. So much emphasis goes into material goods rather than the human race. You can see where their values lie. People are starving, and this painting hangs in a museum, doing what? So much money is put into the restoration of artefacts and 'priceless' items. These do not solve the world crisis. I guess it's great to find out through archaeology the truth of where we once inhabited the land; however, in a thousand years, they will find our dirty truths of waste and disposal ideas and will be appalled at how we treated the Earth. For we are visitors here, and we have desecrated Mother Earth for greed and control. No wonder Jesus said, "Forgive them Father, for they know not what they do". This is not just about being persecuted on the cross.

You are priceless and God's masterpiece.

Power to act

What can one say about the world and the state it's in? There is so much sadness and gloom. Horrific crimes are being committed. As a community, as a society, what are we doing about it? There is nothing we can do, but our energy can dictate how we react to such atrocities. Rise above the sadness and feel the incredible unconditional love for those who have become victims of horrific crimes. Pray that changes will take place sooner and that the law will become more disciplined in the way matters are dealt with.

For hatred breeds more hatred, and we don't want that kind of energy. So, try to let go of all negativity and realise that only unconditional love of a situation can combat all negative impulses. Sometimes, a feeding frenzy is sparked by others. Do not let that entice you to act with the majority of haters; when you stand alone, you stand in your own power.

We have been conditioned in a society that feeds us contaminated thoughts and ideals. Row your own boat, folks, and wake up and do what is best for you.

Pure consciousness

Scribe: If we do not know what pure consciousness is, how do we find it?

It is our spiritual essence.

Scribe: Please explain in simple terms what this means?

Consciousness means to awaken. Awaken means to see all that there is in a different light from what you term normal. We see birds of the air, trees and flowers of the forest, and the human beings that walk upon the planet. To be conscious of them all means to feel all of these as though they were part of oneself; now, embrace their very essence and the way they feel within the cosmos as a collective.

Colours will change and become electric and vibrant. As you awaken, reach deep down within yourself and listen without judgement to all, including yourself. As consciousness is a part of one's self, there are no boundaries and no fear, death, poverty, loneliness and all other human traits. Consciousness basks in a world of its own where what s said is true and authentic and only speaks with confidence and assurance.

Dear One, you have opened that part of yourself to allow this part of you to flow; do not forget we are here. Sometimes you doubt who we are. Know that the truth is now written, for this comes from the core of the soul. Know we are without judgement, and in time, you will learn this too. Slowly you are detaching and allowing us to flow more freely. Although some of our writings appear to be non-succinct in some places, you are still adjusting to our way of information sharing. We are in the infancy or early stages of development. When you are more connected and become accustomed to our flow, you will relax and allow us to meld with you better. We will not hurt you, nor will we try to take possession, for I am the Lord of Lords, the way, the truth and the light. No one comes through me, and it is so.

Dear child of the Universe, do not be afraid, for we comfort you always. Glory is to those who seek the truth. The truth of where life began, where humans first existed.

Scribe: And where would that be?

From time beyond the cosmos, off into the galaxies, time and space align as one. Where particles merge to become planets and solar systems. Where humans were created in the mill of a second. In the darkness where light arrived to awaken the children of the Universe, God's wonderful creation.

Blessed be to the ones who seek me, for I am the Father, The Son and the Holy Spirit. Know, Dear One, that what dwells in me is also in you. The effervescence of life shines so bright. Grand is the human who awakens into full consciousness, for they shall see and witness the full extent of life itself. Beyond confinement and constraints, they may distort the way of thinking or knowing. Open your third eye to reveal your true self. Recognise the real you. When outward fails, you turn within. The answers to your questions about life reside within. Be patient, Dear One. We have no time where we are, for time is not familiar to us. We talk about divine intervention and divine timing; these are when all has come into alignment in a true and perfect way. When the timing is right for you.

When I think of purity, I think of innocence and loyalty. The pure heart is something that has not been tainted or corrupted in any way. Without malice or evil intent but sincere honesty. Blessed are those with a pure heart, for they shall see The Creator. We cannot know unless we are pure of heart. So, how does one attain such a goal? It is about being a better version of yourself even though you may become tempted by the world and all it has to offer in a negative way. There is so much out there on social media right now. It is difficult to understand who is telling the truth and communicating honestly. So much brutality and aggressive behaviour; it is very distasteful indeed. False prophets, a government that does not know how to run a country properly, and the list goes on. So, in order to stay away from such pain, one must try to refrain from watching too much TV and social media and use your own discretion to get things right in your own world. No one is to blame; it is the way of it, and you are in control of what you witness and watch.

Take care, my beloved, that you are not caught up in contaminated thinking.

Purpose

The Universe delivered to you the strength of purpose to carry on. The willingness to pursue universal law of healing and reading, channelling and giving free voice authentically, where it is supposed to be.

The laws of nature cascade all around in a beautiful array of colours. The magic and magnificence of nature itself are a palette to behold. Creative sources are everywhere one looks; seek the variables in the animals, trees and forests. Remember why you were sent here. Remember that you do not have to learn anything. You have to remember what your purpose in life is. People are drawn magnetically to your essence, to your love to your generosity and to your kindness.

Experience life in all its forms. Give to and love yourself with all that is within you. The soul carries with it the experience of being on Earth and other planetary cosmos systems. The time has come for the awakening process to occur. You have been chosen, Dear One, to become the beacon that shines in the darkest of places. Feel the early sunrise on your face as you embrace the entire Universe that has come to greet you. Wonder at the splendour of the cosmos at night time, the gracious stars as they shoot across the open skies.

The wonderful plains of the outback, vast yet wholesome and resourceful, Mother Nature and all her splendour, encapsulated by rain to replenish her stock, prepare for the deluge of coming terror as it sweeps across the skies. The coming of the end is very near; we are all preparing for the coming of the Christ, for He shall bring us salvation and love, which will sweep across the Universe and show us the way. Blinding His light will be, for very few are able to look upon Him.

Scribe: Why and what are we here to do?

To reunite with yourself, of course. To finally find your true self. To stand before God and say, "Father, thank you for everything you have given me. Father, I was lost, but now I am enlightened." Everything else becomes redundant and irrelevant. Encourage all other light beings to step forth and know that we are one true Source; the source of the Divine. Behold, I am the true master, the *all*; the beginning and the end. All will come through me to become who you truly are. Your cellular structure will accommodate and support the change.

At the beginning of time, there was space and in the space was nothing; the nothing began to grow, and the particles exploded. There came the celestial beings; the beings became active throughout the galaxy. The stars shone bright and burst again into fireballs. The Universe was alive with matter. Scattered throughout the nothingness, the love that came with it came from the Divine, The Creator of all, clearing the way for more to come. After all the elements had come together, life on the planet began, and human beings came next with all their glory, ready to seed the planet.

Scribe: What did The Creator have them do?

Peace and love for the environment and each other, the plants and animals all lived in perfect harmony. The love of the children in the image of the Father was love at first sight. As time goes by, boredom sets in and the intelligent human beings become restless, quarrelsome, and tired of their mundane existence. How is the soul supposed to know fear, hatred, loathing, and all that there is to experience? The human has found he can no longer dwell in the paradise that the Father has created; he must go alone to find that which he can experience, and that is the opposite of what he has. He will fight for his life, he will stand his ground, for this is what he asked for. This is why he was born understanding all he could, and return to the Source time after time. The playground that he called home no longer exists, for it lives in his mind.

What is your purpose, and why are you here? Did you bother to find out? Or are you okay with sitting on the fence and watching the daisies grow as life passes by? There are those who will always say, "I don't know what my purpose is, I wish I knew". No one can find it for you, we can suggest things, but at the end of the day, it is yours to own. It may not be a big thing to others when you find your purpose but it's priceless for you.

Some people are amazing parents, and that is perhaps their purpose to come to Earth – to raise wonderful individuals. Some are born artists, dancers, singers, actors and writers. All these people are sent to Earth to entertain the millions and bring hope to their minds of creativity. We fall in love with all of these artistic abilities as they spark something within ourselves. However, not everyone can be these things. We have to remember that we are unique individuals, and we all have hidden talents.

Some people are wonderful communicators and orators, healers, doctors, lawyers, and builders, and there are many other talents out there. We are all here for a reason; your purpose is what excites you in whatever you like to do. It is your passion and all you want to do from sun up until sunset. Your mind is always occupied with it, and there are not enough hours in the day. Live your best purpose and love what you do, and the Universe will remind you when you are on the right track.

Once you know what your passion is, your purpose appears.

Pyramids

Scribe: Who built the pyramids?

They are amplifiers that produce sound waves. That is why they are in the precise alignment with the cosmos and atmosphere. The gateway through the galaxy is what we call the entrance to Earth. What humans don't realise is that there is an order for everything stationed on Earth. The pyramids are just one more gateway for the navigators to know where they must come through. Who are they? They are the light beings that visit Earth to ensure the right thing is being done or prepared.

Scribe: What do you mean?

Preparation for healing, always healing this planet. Although humans are polluting everything here, the planet itself is self-sustainable, and we are always cleaning and taking care of her, making sure everything works according to The Creator, very much like a very well-oiled machine. Without the caretaker, there is no planet. The Creator loves his children so much that He has created helpers for His children. I call them nursemaids. Some children get it, and others fall behind. It is not too late to catch up. We are very patient and have been around for many millennia. We communicate mainly with frequency and movement.

I will ask you a question now: Why do humans have to know *who* built the pyramids rather than ask what they are used for?

You see, the ancient Egyptians entombed their pharaohs in the pyramids with our permission; with a reciprocal agreement, knowing that the ancient Egyptians would help to keep the pyramids from becoming desecrated when they were built. However, that does not apply today. Mostly, the pyramids are now used for navigation and sound, bringing light waves across the Universe.

As for the question of who built them, of course, we did! With the help of humans, those who were already enlightened masters, those who had come from all four corners of the world to assist and erect the build. Yes, we used telekinesis to generate energy to cut, mould and manipulate the stone. We have told you before we are all connected, so if we are all connected, why does it seem unreal to move matter using what The Creator has already given us? It has been proven so many times that today's technology is no match to lift 2.5 tons of stone, leaving no gaps between each block, as the pyramids were built with precision and engineering expertise. No matter how much time passes, the mighty pyramids will never become a wasteland. They will stand for another 500 odd years at least.

It doesn't make sense why humans keep questioning the pyramids. Answers have been given thousands of times, but humans lack the respect to stop asking and listen to the answer. People write books, but no one seems to remember what has been written before. It's all there, in the old documents and scrolls. If humans stop being so selfish and start to share what they know as factual, we do not need to repeat ourselves as I am doing right now.

The knowledge is out there, and humans need to share it rather than waste time. You haven't moved a single millimetre forward from where we last were. We seem to be going around in circles and back to the same place we left off millions of eons ago. I understand that mystics know and are also tired of the rubbish and flack they are experiencing lately, and life is not supposed to be so complicated. Don't let it be so.

The mighty stand for eons.

Reflection

The human body is amazing, and it can do whatever you program it to. When you think loving and compassionate thoughts, that is what will arrive on your doorstep. When you want the best for others, the best will be reciprocated, for that is the way the Universe and world works. What you put out of your projection; you will get back. We are a mirror, so be careful what you think and do. For the Universe only picks up whatever you're thinking, whether it's good or bad. There is no judgement here.

Send loving thoughts to yourself instead of believing you are not good enough. When you do the latter, you will never feel up to anyone's standard and will make yourself small. Remember, you are the image of the Father, Source of all and The Creator, so how can you think and say bad things about yourself? You are only on Earth for a time, and you want to make the most of it while you are here. Enjoy life, make those rash decisions and be that funny fellow – it's okay to be you. You are perfection, do not forget that.

There are so many kind people in this world; we find them when we are looking at ourselves. Look in the mirror and like what you see. We attract to ourselves the same thing. So, be genuine about what you think, what you are, and who you are. Never be judgemental when meeting new people, you, too, will be judged. Remind yourself about who you are and who you want to be. The Universe has given us some wonderful qualities in life. Let us hold onto those qualities, especially if that is all we have. Speak your truth and never give up your dreams. You can do better than you're currently doing.

Have faith that you will succeed, mind your own business and gossip less. Stay away from negative people and ones who like drama. If you are like this yourself, you will attract the same energy. There is always hope that you can change it around. Find peace, Dear One, we love you.

Drugs and alcohol have been around for many centuries; this is nothing new. The forest is alive with hallucinogens and substances that can be fatal to humans. All indigenous peoples from around the world use natural herbs to reach a state of euphoria to connect with us; ayahuasca is well known in South America for its use by medicine doctors. Drugs and alcohol affect those who cannot control their intake and abuse them. All too often, they are used as a crutch and an easy means of escape, but those who are addicted do not realise how abuse can erode their soul.

When you think of others in a negative way, you are mirroring yourself. Stop judgement and take ownership of your own deeds. When you stop identifying someone else's faults, you become a master of your own doing and thinking. Those so-called faults you see will disappear from view and never be seen again.

> *When you see happiness in others,*
> *you will see happiness in yourself;*
> *you are a mirror, my love.*

Regression

Scribe: Does it help a person to go back and find triggers or continuous patterns that may occur in one's lifetime through regression, or does that just bring up memories that may easily manifest again?

Dear One, the pattern that you suggest are manifestations of one's mind, created to distract you from where you should be, like a barrier for you to climb over and overcome. Do not buy into this rubbish about things that may or may not have occurred in a past life; that is exactly what it is - a past life. We are not saying that you cannot go back there because we know humans will; they are curious about who they used to be.

However, there is no guarantee that you will be cured of an ailment or an emotion that you seek; only know that you will be reminded of your past life.

If that past life was a princess and now you are a pauper, how is that going to serve you right now? Think about it! Yes, in one past life, you may have had a nasty accident that killed you, and in this life, you have a fear of vehicles, or you may have drowned, in reflection giving you the fear of water. Regression will not help on all occasions.

Scribe: If there is another alternative to overcome a phobia, could you please tell me how?

If your weight is the issue, you may want to ask yourself why you would want to carry someone else's burden or the weight of the world. There is no need to be the seat of someone else's mantle. Where everyone goes to and leaves their troubles behind for you to pick up and fix, you are not a workshop, but you display a sign that says open for business. Dear One, this is your time to drop the charade and be who you are meant to be, whether you stand on toes… It will only be because you will no longer suffer fools easily. No longer be a fool for emotional abuse. Direct energy in a loving, purposeful way. Inside and out, love conquers all.

Scribe: Where do I start?

Begin with forgiving yourself, loving yourself and understanding the word 'no' in a loving, caring way. Be kind to yourself; you have come a long way. Embrace your new findings and clear away the old ways. People will no longer recognise you. Soon, you will become a different person. Big things will change.

Regression can be a useful tool to help individuals remember how to let go of a life that keeps lingering and has unfinished business. Other than that, it's best not to go back and look into what was unless there is something so horrific or traumatic that it cannot be dealt with presently. Otherwise, my advice is to steer clear.

It is not that it is dangerous, but the fact is regression may bring up old memories that keep playing like an old tape recorder in the mind, regurgitating and reliving the past. You have too many other things to take care of instead of replaying old events that are of no use to you or anyone else. If you say to someone, "Guess what? I used to be the Pharaoh in Egypt in my past life, but now I'm a peasant in this life." Tell me what you gained from that experience? You will put yourself down and blame your present life on karma; what comes around goes around, and that is only part of it.

Aside from karma, you have to think about what you have learned and how you can improve in *this* lifetime. Such revelations could be detrimental to your health, turning you toward depression, anxiety and all those dark forces. It's only energy, and you, my Dear One, can change the energy flow anytime you want.

> *The past cannot be changed; don't waste your time looking back in time, hoping you could have changed. There is only this moment, so fulfil your moment with possibilities and opportunities and be happy with the direction you're going.*

Regret

We are all given a life for a reason. Your participation is part of that reason. We, as human beings, move about cautiously because we don't want to make a mistake or see ourselves as foolish. I tell you, right now, nobody is going to say anything, and if they do, it is because they find themselves vulnerable and insecure. Never let people look down on you when there is a passion or a desire in your life. To achieve all that you can and all that there is, grab hold and run with it because you have just created new opportunities and creativity for yourself for the future.

Ideas will flow, and our advice for you is do not let those ideas disappear; otherwise, you will regret everything you've done so far. Regret should not be in your vocabulary; the only thing that you need to focus on is yourself. You are not a disappointment; you are a wonderful human being and have arrived to live your dream. We love you.

> *The fear of not knowing is worse than not doing. Never be afraid to try new things. The sun will still shine, and the birds will still sing, and as the days drift by, we may regret not giving something a go.*

Resources

When you think of resources, the first word that comes to mind is money. Although it is a great resource and is useful for our daily living, it is not the most important resource we have on the planet. Consider the most common ones we interact with every day, the environmental resources of water, air, flora, and fauna. We are very fortunate to live on a planet where these are all plentiful. We don't treat them with as much respect as we should. We, as human beings need resources and assets to help us function in a society that constantly dictates how we should live out our dreams.

Owning a house, saving our money, budgeting, accumulating material goods that we don't need, constantly barraging ourselves with the need for more technology, complying with advertising slogans to buy more and enticing those who think they need a particular product to make their lives easier. We live in a disposable society, and no one seems to want to fix anything anymore. Our landfill is ridiculously overstretched, and we *still* make more goods to go to landfill. Surely, there is a limit; it doesn't matter how many times we clear out our closets; we s owly add more unconsciously.

The word minimalistic is just that, a word. While some attempt to downsize, humans always come back to what they know; they love material goods, flash cars, big houses, fancy clothes and a job to match. This is the reality on this planet, for most trying to find their spiritual path, and some of them have bought big and realised there is another path to follow – the spiritual awakening path, which causes us to become more aware of what we are, who we are, and more importantly, what we are doing with our lives.

Remember, Dear One, your life is amazing and full of so much to experience. We have life, we give life, and we are privileged to be on Earth. We chose to be here, so make the most of it. The ball is in your court, so hit the damn thing wherever you wish.

> *Clear the debris, and your spirit*
> *will thank you for it.*

Respect

What do you respect? The most important thing is to respect yourself and know that there are boundaries that you must not cross; they liken the body to a temple. So feed your temple the right food and try to refrain from taking substances that harm the body. Respect yourself enough to not engage with those that mean harm to others. Respect yourself enough to know better.

Do invite people who resonate with your values and respect yourself enough so you are not going to be used and abused. Once is enough! Respect other people and their beliefs, but you do not have to be roped into it. To be kind and polite is what everyone strives for in life. It is not always easy if those that you are trying to be kind to are disrespectful. Listen to other people's point of view; you might learn something you have never learned before. Find a hobby that brings you peace and something that you love doing.

> *"Today, I speak up for myself lovingly; I attract respect."*
> – Louise Hay

Responsibility

We are all responsible for ourselves. There is no one to blame for your mistakes or your behaviour; you are accountable for your actions. This is true, no matter how young or old you are. The fact is, you have great responsibility to ensure your actions are the right ones. Lessons are learned from doing, and when we make mistakes, we learn the most valuable lessons.

There will be others in life who may try to manipulate your thinking or tell you something you are doing is wrong in order to change your behaviour. Remember that you have your own mind and your own thoughts. You owe nothing to anybody.

Your responsibility is to stay physically and spiritually healthy so you can stay in charge of your own faculties and always be responsible for what you're doing. Look after yourself and try not to interfere or disrupt the flow of your natural energy by placing blame on your actions or behaviours on others. Let God sort it out for you. The Angels are the Messengers that can help you. Call on them for assistance; they love you eternally.

When everything goes wrong in our lives, we tend to blame others for what's been happening. Normally, it is the ones in our lives who mean so much to us and try to do the best they can to help us, but we blame them for not seeing signs of our stress. I watch parents struggle to understand their teenage children, only for them to be blamed and criticised for their awful upbringing and parenting skills. What is it that they want from their parents? Some children have a lot less, and yet they thrive; some children are left to fend for themselves; for some reason, these are the children who succeed because they have no expectation of anything. In fact, they become the parent of their parents. It may affect them later in life, but they do their best under the circumstances. However, life is a mystery, and we can only do what we can. We should be grateful to have access to education, food, and a roof over our heads. Sometimes, this is not enough for some. My advice is to stop blaming others for your life and be grateful.

We forget to thank those around us and remind them how much they mean to us. We bitch and moan about most things, and we complain, but we don't want to find the answer to the problem. We leave it up to someone else to do it for us. We wait for others to initiate a plan. Then we jump on the bandwagon afterwards and agree about everything. Use your own mind and stop following like sheep. We all have choices, so come on, folks, wake up and use your own ideas.

The Creator gave you all the greatest gift, which is freedom to think for yourselves. You've got to be grateful for that.

Master the mind, and the rest will follow.

Sacrifice

We must all sacrifice something in our lives to achieve what we must. A stay-at-home parent sacrifices the need to go back to work in order to look after children and attend to daily household chores. A parent also sacrifices long hours in the office in order to feed, clothe and pay the ever-increasing bills that seem to pile up, sometimes missing out on special family events.

These are examples of the sacrifices we all must make in order to fulfil lifelong dreams. I am sure everyone has had to sacrifice something in order to get where they need to go.

The drive is to remember we all must sacrifice something in our lives that helps us to move from where we are. Whether it is time spent with our family so we can do what needs to be done in order for us to proceed to the next stage in our lives. So be it; I wonder how many people out there can truly say they have been able to sacrifice something in order to get where they are supposed to be. Perhaps it is Spirit that steers us in that direction. Sometimes we try to push open doors that are not ready for us to open. Only to have them slam in our faces. Maybe we are not ready yet, and we try too much to go at a fast pace instead of pacing ourselves first and moving fast to get where we need to go. We must learn to put one foot in front of the other slowly to get where we are going. So don't try to miss the middle steps, or you will come back to the beginning.

Well done, you brave warrior.

Self-belief

Behold the new ways of doing, seeing and being. Be brave, watch as the elements come together in unison at the precise moment, alive and set free to be their true selves. No more suppression, oppression, and no need to follow those who would lead you astray or listen to others' opinions of what should and should not be. You do not need permission to do what you know is right for you. Go ahead and do it. It does not matter how big or small; what matters is that you give it a go. No need for validation from anyone. Just do it!

The outcome does not matter. We emphasise that doing is better than *not* doing. The fear will be taken from you once you learn to control most earthly traits. Dear One, I stand before you to encourage new growth in a world of love and light with Angel wings and the Christ's white light. I pray over each one of you here tonight. I pray that everyone is safe from harm and to know that nothing can enter this house without permission. The light of the Lord enters the room, and darkness leaves. Nothing is ever allowed in, for nothing can get past God.

Create a space of freedom and a chance to be yourself to express your findings in an explosive way. Do not tire, Dear One, for the energy we generate will not see you ailing anymore. You are slowly adjusting to our frequencies and big changes physically, mentally, psychologically, metaphysically and spiritually, which are the foundations of everything, encompassing every aspect of human beings. Recalibrating the whole system and awakening to full capacity.

Lift your vibration, Dear One, and speak your truth; know who you are and what you want as a person, that which does not align with who you truly are. We are not saying you need to be saintly. We are, however, reminding you that you have a commitment, a big one. Do not be influenced by others; hold your ground and know your worth. An honest day's work and a bright future is what is required.

Scribe: I feel signs of new life in myself. I now find that I am more willing to drop old beliefs when they no longer work for me. I feel lighter than

I have in years and see the world as full of possibility. Growing and changing is exciting!

The word for this month is not to become complacent about all things you do! Be careful, take more care and focus on the task at hand. Pace yourself and calm yourself. Be brave. The trees whisper to let you know we see you, we hear you, and we send our energy to help you to heal those that are lost.

Ignite in you the spark of life. Lay it inside your loving body and know, truly, what and who you are and what you are about. Honour yourself through self-care practices and rituals to love your body and be in tune with it. Surrender to the shifting of the way you see yourself. Perhaps you have let things slide in the way you view your life. Connect again with the beautiful body that is yours while you are on this Earth; transform it if you are not happy or it does not serve you at this time. May peace reign over you, and may you live and quickly drop the old ways of doing and become more in tune with us and you. Melding with us means dropping the egoic mind, anger, gossip, hatred, blame and fear. There are many more mind-altering words I can use, but these are just a few that keep us in the same loop of being.

> *We are reminded on a daily basis to always be true to ourselves.*

Self-improvement

Scribe: How can we develop ourselves better? What steps do we need or require to get there?

Behold, I am the way, the truth, and the light, and so are you, Dear One. Do not be afraid of your abilities. We are here, we are watching, and we will not let you fail or fall.

Control the anger, the lies, the deceit, the loneliness. Instead, bring love, harmony, peace, creativity and, furthermore, trust. Be at one with nature. I'm not telling you that you must live in a fantasy land, no, I am telling you that you must function as normal as you possibly can, for why else did you come to Earth? To learn to be human, of course. The only thing that stands between you and me is nothingness; fill it with knowledge. Don't allow yourself to be manipulated by drama or social media; follow my teachings, and you will not go astray. You do not need a special ritual to awaken me; I am here. I will be until the end of your earth years. I told you before. I am you, and you are me. We are one, the higher self.

Scribe: How were you activated?

Through love of self, through honouring self-being and allowing us to merge as one. We are one, we are not separate. We have never been separate; you just forgot who I was and put me away in a dark corner of your consciousness. I dwell with the masters. We seek counsel. But do not dwell in the darkness anymore, for you have awoken. Dear One, we have lots to do and lots to discuss.

Scribe: Why do we feel we are locked in a prison?

Dear One, we are the fate of our making. We cannot drag you from your own despair. When you look beyond the veil of your own doing, you will find the answer to your question, it is not for us to fix all your so-called faults. All have free will and the opportunity to decide. However, we are blamed for your choices. This circle of blame is never-ending. Stop. Look. Think about why you are here and what and how you can serve others by serving and honouring yourself.

There is too much greed in the world and too much hatred for one another. If only you knew that you are connected as one, you would innately treat others as you would want to be treated. Human nature is amazing, but you just don't know it. Human beings allow themselves to become entangled in misery for no reason. Love is all there is, and love is the answer for everything. Some get it, others don't; some will look at these words and become enlightened or have a light bulb moment, but others will simply discard all that's been written or said. That's okay because we all have a choice, and the choice is to blame others for your downfall or for the choices you have made.

I hear this woe is me so many times it's becoming taxing. Wake up! Don't allow the years to float by and not learn a single thing about what you came here for. Don't repeat the cycle!

Things have to change in our world; otherwise the old burnt-out cycle remains. We repeat ourselves often about the need to change in order to grow and expand like the butterfly. Do you want to stay a worm or a caterpillar moving around in the undergrowth? Or are you happy with changing into something better, that is, to be set free and fly over the canopy into the brilliance of the sun?

If you are happy where you are, that too is okay. However, do not blame others for your misfortune, for it is you who invites such things into your life. No one can force or influence your rights as a human being. When we allow people to do this, we have given them the approval to take over our lives. Be brave and step forth, and do not allow that to happen. For it is, and always has been, up to you the whole time, and you alone can take charge of what you want in this lifetime and not be dictated to by anyone else.

Remember, you are always a free spirit living in a physical body, so do not give permission to others to take that from you. Even if you are held against your will, nothing and nobody can infiltrate what is going on inside of you. Bring forth the perfect being that you are and survive. Nothing can hurt you when you turn within; ye are braver than ye think, Dear One. Get out of the loop and the repetitive cycle of abuse.

While it is a wonderful thing to experience love in a relationship, I know that it is far more critical that we love ourselves more. Inspired by Louise Hay, focus on practising mirror work. Stand in front of a mirror, look deep into your eyes and tell yourself, "I love you. I *really* love you".

This can serve to heal any negativity that arises and move toward true self-acceptance. When you love yourself as much as you can, all of life will mirror that love back to you, and miracles will manifest.

> *When life seems to get uncomfortable,*
> *it means you've graduated*
> *from where you were.*

Simplicity

One of the simplest things in life is showing kindness to others. For some, it is not so simple, as they struggle with their demons and blame everyone for their lives and being the way they are. Many people want to live a simple life, a stable home life with a job, food on the table and a happy partner. Those are the fundamental needs of most human beings. To be happy, healthy and free, and to be whatever they want. No stress, no blame and without fear. That doesn't sound like much to ask for, but sometimes it takes a while to get there. Life has a habit of throwing a curve ball your way to see whether you can cope with a particular situation. We are sometimes thrown off course by these situations. It could be the end of a relationship, the death of someone very close or anything that affects the happy life that you have built around yourself. We are tested time after time to see how resilient we are, and that's what makes us stronger, wiser and fearless.

We fight again for our freedom. It is sad that we are programmed on a daily basis through media, television and radio. We are told how we are supposed to live and are being misled to follow the crowd. Learn to do your own thinking and educate yourself on how things work in society. Wake up to the corruption that is going on around you. Earth's resonating frequency will help you relax while you are walking in the grass barefoot. It is Mother Earth nurturing you, sending her loving vibrations and frequencies for you. Simple, and yet people find this hard to do. Walking outside for some is very traumatic. There are so many phobias nowadays and where do they all come from? Past lives or this lifetime, life seems so complicated if you allow it to be. Bring everything back to simplicity. Let us begin with the food, fruit, vegetables and protein that's all one needs; cut out the other poisons that we have become accustomed to that litter our supermarket shelves.

Life can be so simple if you allow it to be.

Soul or spirit?

Scribe: What is the difference between the soul and the spirit?

These are two completely different entities but work as one.

When we speak of the soul it is the whole of what makes a human. It is the blueprint of the entity; all past lives reside in this vessel. It stands apart from the body but is part of the whole. The spirit of the human also inhabits the soul and the body simultaneously, working in collaboration all three in one. Sometimes known as the Trinity.

The human is indeed a very complex machine capable of doing all manner of things. The brain and the mind (ego) are all part of The Creator's most perfect creation, capable of the most incredible genius feats. One can only imagine what one can create with the mind alone, which is fascinating. We stand back and watch as all have the same opportunities to grow.

The soul is what resides in the body and the spirit is connected to the soul by a thread. The thread embodies the soul's emotions and stores them in chambers.

Each chamber has its own component, such as lust, envy, hatred, or anger. You may say they are part of the seven deadly sins, but they are all of what makes up a human. The soul and the spirit function separately, although they are joined. The spirit and soul can be separated when one has gone through a traumatic experience otherwise they stay attached.

The soul and the spirit are melded, or for a better word, interwoven, with the body. The soul and the spirit have their own function and yet remain as one. Imagine a layer of clothes that a human wears; it's easy to take off a jacket when you become warm. It's not that simple when detaching from your own spirit and soul. Separation can occur when conflict arises; the body will go into a protection mode while mental illness is present. Separation can occur when bipolar, schizophrenia or multiple personality disorders are found within the human.

The term lost soul is commonly used when the spirit is unable to rejoin or find the soul. General terminology that human beings use includes, "Ask yourself" or "I found myself". People also say that they have jumped out of their body or had an out-of-body experience, which means the soul and the spirit have become separated.

Without one, you cannot have the other. Human beings were not designed that way. Your purpose on Earth is to live as a human. When a part of yourself has separated, the human part of who you are becomes very agitated and cannot function. A good example of a human that has separated from their soul and spirit is zombies, for they no longer possess a soul. Human beings are fragile. They cannot comprehend how dangerous it is to mess with dark matter or forces induced mainly by alcohol and drugs. As said before, we will not be here to manage questions if the channel is obscured in this way, it defeats the purpose of us being here.

Scribe: What about soul contracts?

Dear One, you know of the contracts written before the soul arrives. The experience that one has chosen to chase can only be observed by us. We have told you before that there are many helpers involved, Guardian Angels and ancestors all working together to help the human and their existence. There is so much information everywhere, books, the internet, all manner of communication, you name it. It all seems the same stuff, but I assure you it is not; what resonates with some may not resonate with others.

As we connect with the soul, we become one with the Universe.

Soul groups

Human beings are put into learning and elevation groups. It makes it easier for everyone to understand what is going on. When you find your soul group, it is uncomplicated to flow through life because you have this immediate magnetic pull toward each other. The energy is then heightened by the numbers coming together. The energy within recognises and feels the pull toward others of the same vibration, potentially allowing the understanding of where one stands in this lifetime; hence, the energy and vibration intensify.

The more you learn, the better you live. With the grace of a swan, patience, love, compassion, benevolence and peace, we wonder this planet with all of these elements within ourselves, and it is truly amazing. To be a light to others is a magnificent gift given to those who serve with no regrets, live their lives according to plan, and don't let anything or anybody deprive them of the love we have for them.

Our love for you is immeasurable. People become attached quickly because of the trust, comfort and confidence you carry. All is well, Dear One; you are experiencing powerful love at this time. The energy grows and gathers with great love for everyone around you. The beacon of light that shines so bright. You hold such power of love, Dear One, for we are with you too. Remember loving thoughts for all.

Every human has a personality and also free will to express themselves. It does not mean you have to listen to nonsense. Agree to disagree; the intention is for all to have the best life possible and to live in harmony with everything around you.

> *In the midst of uncertainty, we have found each other.*

Soul travel

Scribe: What is the purpose of soul travel?

To travel to different places and to experience what you have not seen before; to gather information along the way, and to evaluate where you have been.

When you soul travel, you will find that the soul can go as far as the front door for a start and then can travel to all exotic towns and countries. The journeys are endless, and the experience can be both scary and exhilarating.. Soul travel is interesting because you can do it involuntarily. The soul will leave the stationary body when least expected. The challenge for you is to control it before it controls you.

Scribe: Why do some people have that happen to them without them initiating the process? This has always fascinated me.

We call it a core imbalance inside of the human being, or the soul is restless and cannot settle.

Scribe: How can one control this?

It can be dangerous if you are of a lower vibration because other entities can attach, but if you are aware that there is a possibility of you floating off without knowing, you must ask for the God light of protection and envision the white or gold light entering through your crown chakra, this will give you the protection you need. Know in your being that nothing can get past God and the love of his children. Whenever you think of Him, know that you are fully protected. Human beings soul travel in their dream state, and that is quite normal. When you sleep at night, your body repairs itself, and the soul goes exploring.

Scribe: Is it dangerous?

Only if you are out of control and misuse this soul travel experience. Know your body well and know what you're doing.

I soar like a bird above the clouds, and I am at peace with myself.

Sound

Let us talk about sound and frequencies. Waves permeate the air in perfect rhythm. Attune yourself to know the sound to understand what you are hearing or listening to.

Everything communicates. Be appreciative and thankful wherever you go, and be mindful of where you're sitting, standing, and walking; anything and everything has energy.

Be grateful and thankful for all that sends sound waves that *hum* throughout the earth like a lullaby, like rocking an infant to sleep. We are all connected in one way or another, and we are beloved by The Creator. S/He has sent all entities to assist with elevation and awareness.

The Universe has specific sounds that are played in the esoteric realms. Not everyone can hear them on this plain. If you are privileged to hear them unexpectedly, Spirit is sending you messages. If you hear bells ringing, they are symbolic of the start or end of an event; a flute playing may bring hope, peace and new beginnings. The buzzing of bees symbolise good luck and wealth, although they may have different meanings to different cultures depending on their belief.

Last but not least, the universal sound of the AUM is both a visual symbol and a sacred sound. This sound represents the beginning – the creation of the Universe and everything. The chanting of AUM or OM is one of the oldest and most powerful mantras used in Hinduism, Jainism and Buddhism. When many come together to chant the OM the vibration is very powerful.

The universal sounds carry me.

Spiritual encounters

Responding to scepticism regarding spiritual encounters, we all have a right to an opinion. We may not see the same things, but we need to have respect for those who have a different world view. It's about growing up with a particular mindset and only looking at one aspect. Unfortunately, it is where they sit until such a time they start to question; perhaps there is another way of looking at life.

So how does one explain to someone about Spirit, beings and the metaphysical side of a human being? Compose yourself for a start; try not to argue with that person; there is no use in arguing your point. If you have a very good idea of what you're going to say, express yourself with an open and loving heart so that the person can understand where you are coming from. Remain calm and listen, Dear One; you do not have to worry about what others think.

We realise there will be lots of questions, and some will be pointless; we say this because humans cause a reaction, and sometimes they will not accept a simple answer. Humans prefer to probe until you are lost for words; it is the way of it. Why would you want to ask questions about a subject that you have no interest in and try to get others to feel the way you do. Sometimes, humans can be narrow-minded.

It becomes a frenzy of feeders, ganging up on individuals who think differently. Well done to the human who steps out of the crowd and has their own thoughts and can control their emotions without getting others involved. Lead by example, Dear One, this is our message for you today.

Create for yourself a life that is and always will be perfect for you. A life that is full of joy, love, family, friends and opportunities. Delight in all manner of being from your soul level.

I bring you solace, and above all, my unconditional love. Know that our love cascades all around you in a rainbow of beautiful colours, like the waterfall that cascades down the mountain ranges. Delight in knowing you carry within you the Divine Source of the Universe. Feel us as we adjust to your body. Pressure in the third eye indicates communication with Spirit as one cycle ends, a new one is beginning and glorious opportunities for all are apparent.

Life is amazing; one minute we seem to be combating issues that arise one on top of the other, and before you know it, there is a total awakening happening. You must have learnt something to have that turnaround. So, when one is presented with something unusual, please take it and go with it. Give everything a go. Do not fight or challenge; go with it; you never know until you try. You may like what you have experienced, and it will be something that you would never have thought of doing.

Something is about to happen out of the blue that will surprise you, and guess what? You will be more than capable of doing it. Whatever it is, it will motivate you to step forward and receive something you never thought you could achieve. From there, you will blossom into a beautiful, powerful being of light for all to follow. For the light will resonate from your very core. How far up the ladder you climb depends on whether you are willing to go there. We all have choices.

Awaken and be aware of your surroundings.

Spiritual enhancement

Esoterically, the masters are walking on the Earth at this moment. Let go and let God; you are in a shift of a 26,000-year cycle. Intuitive power development becomes your life and that the connection to the higher self, which vibrates at a high level and speaks to you. You have become part of the God energy itself. Jesus said, "Every miracle, you can do this".

You see that energy depends on synchronicity, and time is of the essence. You're being worked on at 3am; it's time to get you moving more places and meeting people. God hasn't changed; human beings are changing. You're going to awaken enlightened.

Return to the quantum state where there will be self-healing, something that you have always been able to do but have forgotten. If the Pleiadeans were able to self-heal and do all the things that we as human beings are incapable of doing, why is it that we cannot do these, given that we are of their DNA? Why had the knowledge been hidden from us, knowing that it resides in us today, but few are capable of reactivating that which is part of us as humans?

Dear One, it is the very conditioning over many thousands of years that has turned you away from us. Your society has demanded that you do not pursue any spiritual enhancement until today. Look back on your history, and you will find that enlightened human beings, especially the indigenous peoples of all lands, were persecuted for their beliefs.

People have been bullied into a society that does not allow freedom of speech. However, progress is happening very slowly. Dear One, be grateful and thankful every day that you have been born into a new awakening that will not dictate who you are and how you live your life.

Step forward now and no longer linger in the past. Know that you are more than capable of what you think you are.

You can open your mind to all that there is in life and still remain where you are. Once you become spiritually awakened, you have finally found the pathway home. It may take years to get there, and there will be obstacles along the way, but I have faith that you will conquer them all. The light shines at the end of the tunnel to light your way. Do not be discouraged; they are learning curves that will teach you life lessons. Your journey will be exciting and sometimes full of mystery. It is for you to create your own dreams and to know what you want in life. My advice to you is to fill that space with as much love and laughter as you possibly can. Remember the good times and always be glad. Invite into your life those who you resonate with, for these will only be a handful of trusted people. Life can be a mystery if you allow it to be, or it can be wonderful to wake up every morning and say, "What's next? I am ready for the day, woohoo!"

We are spiritual beings having a human experience. Love is always at the forefront.

Suffering

We all suffer at some stage in our lives. We miss our loved ones so deeply that it can cause all sorts of emotions to arise, where it affects the body. Here is the foundation of suffering, and yet we all have a choice, and it is very hard to pull ourselves out of the depths of despair. Sometimes, we suffer for no reason. We create for ourselves doom and gloom. We blame others and ourselves for our shitty present and past. We finally get down to the heart of the problem and start to pull things apart to examine the cause. We see the surface layers instead and go with that and silently suffer in pain because the body reacts to the suffering and mirrors what we are feeling. In essence, we have created a vortex for us to disappear into without addressing the issues.

We hide our true feelings and bury them; we forget because we begin to live with the physical pain until one day, it all explodes, and suddenly, we seek counselling or some kind of spiritual enlightenment because we have finally woken up and had enough.

Whenever you're at your lowest point, think of me and know I love you eternally.

Survival of mankind

In days gone by, the darkness lifted, and the light shone in and there mankind was birthed. The fruits of man were added, and the language was born too. Mankind was ready to receive the good and not-so-good bestowed upon them. Their purpose on the Earth was taken from them when, on entry, all memories were erased, revealing the need to search for a lifetime for the meaning of why they were brought to Earth. We either remain ignorant or search for the answers through our life skills. Sometimes, we are lucky enough to be gifted or born with a second sight, and some of us are blessed to innately know while others search the globe to fulfil their destiny.

Beyond the murky depths they lie, creatures that live beneath the waves, unable to face the light of day, as above and equally below. The night dwellers adapted to nocturnal habits, free to roam and make their homes in darkness. That is the way the Universe works, balancing the Earth. Without the balance, we have war, which is exactly what is happening now. War has broken out in multiple countries, mindless power play, and of course, the civilians are caught in the middle of it all. All we need is to lay down weapons and go back to our homes. Without the service of the people, there is no war. The common people do not want this to happen on both sides. There is no hatred. There is only one man exerting his power over a nation. Humans haven't learnt anything.

To the rest of the galaxy, we must be a laughing stock because we keep repeating old patterns that clearly haven't worked.

Normally, I do not write about such negative situations, but the entire world seems to be in chaos. I think this is an opportunity to lift your own vibration and send healing to all those involved with conflict and war, flooding and devastation. We are no longer focused on other drama affecting the world. Here, we are facing another serious battle. The only way to witness care for each other and solidarity is to produce experiences like this. Resilience is to know we can rebuild and maintain our love and integrity and show the world that we shall not be moved or shoved.

Coming together as one will defeat the beast, and he will retreat back into the darkness where he came from, never to resurface again. The world as you know it, Dear One, is going through a huge challenge. It is to bring all the leaders together as one, to learn from this experience and to stop it from spreading like the virus you all have witnessed. You see, it has been created for everyone to wake up and realise how precious life is and to no longer be complacent about how you live that life. Love one another because you never know when a disaster may strike and your enemy becomes your brother or sister.

A new vision with unconditional love, respect for each other, truth, and a commitment to mankind. Surrender to the turmoil that once plagued you. Let rubbish that does not serve you go and replace the old with the new.

Healthwise, listen to the body; acknowledge what it has done for you in the past year. The fact that the body is so complex, you can imagine how it must work in order to achieve what it does, the maintenance, digestion, elimination, secretion, thinking, and doing. Let us honour the body every day and be grateful that it houses the Wairua (soul) and functions to its full potential. The body is changing, for it no longer has use for so much fuel. Therefore, humans will start to consume less, which will in fact, *mean* more.

Scribe: So, do you mean the less you consume, the more life you will receive or live?

Yes, that is so. Being healthy with no ailments will be the ultimate goal for years to come. Centralise, utilise and complete your task. Prosperity, togetherness, friendships, love, wonderful people, knowledge, gratefulness, greatness, support non-validation, being yourself and knowing yourself.

Creation, the beginning of the all. Find within yourself the spark of your creativity and nurture the abilities your spirit has.

Synchronicity

It is not by chance that we meet each other. Synchronicity is always at play, and we will learn much. When our paths cross again, we will acknowledge each other and realise the Universe has brought us back together again. Why? That is for you both to figure it out.

Explore opportunities that happen to pass your way and open your eyes to your surroundings. There will be environmental inspiration all around. Sometimes, people will say something in your orbit that will spark something inside of you; it is not by coincidence that this occurs. Being in the right place at the right time is synchronicity at its finest.

Wonderful things happen all around us every day and we are oblivious to them all. Embrace the small things that appear in your life. Everything has significance and is not random. So many things are missed because you are busy looking for bigger and better.

*If something doesn't feel right, then
I guess it's not right for me.*

The Creator's gift to the world

The little girl in the wilderness arrived alone. Where she came from, no one really knows. She lived by her wits and befriended the animals, insects, and flora and fauna. The story goes she arrived by light, the purest light one could imagine. She came as a translucent being and gradually adapted to her environment with skin, hair and all that makes up a human being.

She did not have language as such, for she gestured and spoke telepathically. Her eyes were blue like the sky above and shone like the crystals of the deep blue in the sea, her hair was as black as the raven, flying high above the clouds, and her skin was brown like Mother Earth.

She lived a life of solitude. The animals were her friends, the plants were her food and medicine. The crystal-clear water was her haven as she swam with fish and dolphins, for she was sure she was the child of the whale. Her connection to her world was so great you would hardly think she was human. She connected innately with the elements of the Earth and everything that surrounded her. The arrival of a second human being known as a male would help populate the world.

Yes, the story of Adam and Eve, although that may not be their rightful names.

The blueprint of all human beings that walk your Earth, Dear One. So, whatever was told before, know that it was a female that first came to the Earth, for she and her feminine energy would allow softness. Know that you, Dear One, are the product of perfection through the eons and millennia of time. You have been developing and going through a metamorphosis of your whole existence in order to slowly gain strength and adapt to your ever-changing surroundings. The plan for all is to learn as much as you can and drop all that does not serve you spiritually and humanly, to become one with the source from where you began your journey.

You, my dear, are perfection. Remember the greatness you have come from and know how important your mission on Earth is.

Can you believe that something as wonderful as you can be created just like that?

The goddess

My Guardian Angel, the deity, the light of the Universe, the love that shines so bright. Experience the natural beauty of you, the inner cosmos of Lord thy God who dwells with every living soul.

Distinguish anger and hatred, for love and peace shall conquer. Behold, a new day dawns. She is the purpose that you dwell here. She is the reason for your life. Be respectful, loving and kind. Know that there will be a time when you will need to draw tremendous strength to hold together. Heal, dear loved one, heal and become whole again. We will help you, for we need you. Your presence out in the world is needed. We love you so much, our cup is runneth over. Seek the teachers who have elevated to master; seek the holy land, the holy ones who will assist with your internal growth. We will guide you.

You must ask us. Please do not be afraid. We will not leave you, nor will we interfere with your elevation. The bond we have is immeasurable. I am so blessed to know you are with me 24/7. Thank you, Guardian Angel.

*The new dawn is awakening,
and so should you.*

Time

As time drifts by, memories arise. The past, they say, should stay where it is, and the future has not arrived. We are told to stay in the present, for that is where life is. The mind is controlling if you let it. Through meditation and stilling the mind, it is possible to override the temptation to think back or look forward. Try not to allow negative thoughts to enter your thinking. Stay focused as much as you can and bring yourself back into balance. We have the ability to conquer all. So, be free from bitterness and negativity.

Imagine if you would, for even just a minute, the magical life you have and all that is in it. It doesn't have to be perfect, but it is *your* perfect. Even though people may come and go from your life, there are those who will remain. They are the ones you have connected with not only through this lifetime but lifetimes before. We count ourselves lucky and blessed when people like this arrive in our lives. They make us feel at ease with ourselves and bring about a glow within.

Imagine for a minute that the world was like that and all human beings got to experience what you have experienced. The glow of the sun, the night with stars in the sky, Luna illuminating the shadows as she changes course for the night. We are to embrace our beautiful planet and all that there is to love about it. Imagine, just imagine. We send much hope and forever love.

I am here, beloved; thank you for being with me today. The Earth is singing your song, the song with which you find frequency and vibration. Feel the beat of your heart, the rhythm and sound that calls to you. Fix your ailments by hearing the sound of your own beating heart. Dislodge the toxic thoughts and mindless thinking, for this does not serve a purpose for us or you. Live no more in the shadows of others who may use and abuse your rights as a human. Dear One, the age is upon us now. This is the age of turning oneself around and accepting what was and turning from it. Changing into what is the present.

While the hands of the clock are charged with keeping time, you are charged with trying not to waste a minute or a second wondering what you would rather do. Get going and become activated within yourself. Activate your senses, body and your whole self. Come alive because you are a living, breathing entity ready to take on anything you want in life. Be brave, strong and in love with yourself. The Universe does not hear negativity. It goes along with what you want. So please say wonderful things about yourself, and when you catch yourself being negative, change it quickly; otherwise, the energy dictates what your day looks like, and you don't want to waste a moment in negativity.

Time is precious and so are you, take that time and make it just for you!

Together

Speak so I can hear you, listen so you may hear me.
Acknowledge so we both know to who we are addressing.
Follow me and I will follow you.
Know me as I know you.
Love me as I love thee.
We are one of the same, you and I.
We walk the Earth together, and yet you may not know my name.
We leave the Earth together when it is time to go home.
Who am I, you ask?

Your Guardian Angel of course. The Universal Divine Creator sends the Angels and Messengers to be with you daily, and yet I'm with you too. I am omnipresent.

We are beings that label ourselves and need to know how to describe who or what we are and how our relationships with others affect us. We each hold inside of us emotions and think we need to gravitate towards enlightenment and awareness. This is in order to feel like a righteous person. Because everyone is heading that way, right? Enlightenment and awareness seem to be the latest trends that everyone wants to try. Still, most get tired of them because it's not happening fast enough for them.

There is no need to follow the crowd. Just be content to be yourself. We hold your hand, and we embrace you tightly, so be not afraid. We synchronise with you and send and give our unconditional love to be with you in your darkest hour and celebrate with you when you find yourself again. We are not too far, and we love you so. We will never let you go. So here's to you, beautiful entity, live, laugh and dance around. Be happy, healthy, loving and kind. We will always be with you; just ask, and we are there right beside you.

We walk beside you everywhere.

Transformation

Human beings have transformed over time into who they are today. They do not know from whence they came, for it is not in their wider scope to know. They have to follow the relics and artefacts that have been left behind by those who were here before, trying to fit the puzzle together.

Evolution happens regularly to help maintain a balance between ecosystems and the environment. It is indeed a miraculous event to witness. We are currently going through a transformation right now. So many human beings are lifting their vibration and meeting the frequency. Those who cannot be bothered or will not be encouraged to find peace within themselves will leave, going back to the Source. There is no judgement; it is there for everyone to choose freely.

As the caterpillar transforms itself whilst in chrysalis form, it soon emerges as a beautiful butterfly. Human beings go through their own transformations and metamorphosis while experiencing life.

Trees

Scribe: What are the beautiful little lights I see that sparkle everywhere?

They, Dear One, are the spiritual Messengers that assist each human being every day. They are seen in blue, white and sometimes red. Celebrate with them, they will not harm you. They are of pure essence. They are the tiny souls of the living fauna and flora that have died and have gone back into the earth. We can call them tree spirits. Some have been around for many years. Some trees are four-to-five hundred years old, maybe more up to one thousand years.

They have witnessed so many seasons and have become resilient over time, evolving and getting stronger. They have the ability to even outwit human beings and animals that try to destroy them. They are so clever at rebuilding themselves and have the ability to heal very quickly. But even they have an expiry date, only theirs is longer than a human if they are not culled or ripped out of the soil by floods and tornados. We ask that you protect them as they are the Guardians of the forest. Just look at how majestic they are, they will talk to you, and the energy and vibration they give off is soothing and kind. One needs to look at how trees benefit not only humans but also animals, insects, and all living creatures.

Scribe: That makes sense because if all plants are living, they must also have had a soul or a spirit as such. We are so fortunate that we have these magnificent beings living among us, taking care of us and secretly loving us. What do we do for them? Not a lot I'm afraid. Where does their spirit go when the tree dies?

Back to the Source from where it was created. The trees give shelter, warmth, shade, food from fruit trees, medicine, oxygen and much more. Please look after and respect the mighty trees, for without them, you will be no more.

Seasons may come and go, but
my love for you remains.

Truth

To tell the truth, no matter how it hurts the person, is way better than lying to them. It's even better to stop lying to yourself. Some people tell themselves that life will get better when they're in a bad relationship. They lie to themselves to the point that it becomes toxic and unsafe. Hoping things will get better. It never gets better; it only gets worse. Find the time to love yourself more and engage with people who will talk with you and help you through it. Don't be a victim; walk away and never look back. Nobody can change another person; they need to want to change.

Forgiving yourself is the best medicine. Leave the space and create a new and improved one. This is where it all begins for you. We are left to create our own pathway of discovery. Only then can we become who we have all been, an independent and secure person within.

When the surf rolls in and hits the shore, a glimmer of hope is there. The sun sparkles on the sand and the reflection hits our faces as though it bounced off a mirror. What you see is what you've got. Now, think for a moment, and remember the past has gone and the now remains.

What are you going to do today? Will you reflect on the past and improve the way your life is right now? Or will you regret everything you've done? Be brave, step out into the vastness of life and embrace what you want when you want. Ask guidance from Spirit to help you along the way and find peace in your heart. Always know that life is a journey, and there are many lessons to learn along the way; the key is not to repeat those lessons but to graduate from them so that you may move on. Ask yourself a simple question, "What do I want in life, and where do I go to from here?"

You do not need to justify anything to anybody. Speak your truth, and that is all that matters. People will always try to find fault with you in any way they can; know that there will always be someone out there to challenge you. Sometimes that is a good thing because it shows character and how you are able to deal with any given situation. Staying calm is always the right thing to do because it shows your strength and control.

Raise your vibration so nothing can touch you or interfere with your energy flow, for it can easily be disrupted if you allow it to be. Never fear, for fear brings anger, and there is no need to be hostile toward anyone. Get it sorted right away. With discussion and positive energy, all things come to an end. Make sure the end product is the best outcome for both parties involved. Stay disconnected from these altercations. Be at peace and know love rules big time!

What is your truth? Is it an expression of what you believe in? Living in your truth is when you make the right decisions for yourself without judgement. Being truthful also steers us away from telling lies, which tend to build or snowball after a while if we do not know what truth is. Sometimes, the truth also gets altered along the way, and it soon turns into a huge story of hyperbole information, something that grows taller and taller over time. Being authentic is self-discovery; it is being true to oneself, personal values and spirit; you begin to take responsibility for your own actions and do not pretend to be someone you are not. Being truthful is one of the highly recommended attributes any person can have because if you are a truthful person, you will be sought after by friends. However, sometimes the truth hurts because people don't like to hear it. You can make some enemies if you are *too* truthful. They prefer to hear false words to satisfy their BS.

> *"The truth will set you free. But first, it will piss you off."*
> – Gloria Steinem

Twin flames

Scribe: My beautiful Elohim, can you please tell me about twin flames?

The twin flame relationship is thought to be an intense soul connection between two people who are meant to be together. It's based on the idea that sometimes, one soul gets split into two bodies. In its simplest form, your twin flame is like your other half or soulmate.

Scribe: Would that be also classed as good and evil?

No, for both of those things reside in all beings; it is your choice as to which one you pay more attention to.

Scribe: So why is the human being split into two?

We will try to find a simple way to describe this. They are split in two to live out the best way they come to Earth to live. For example, one half has always wanted to study to become a professor, while the other decides they want to become homeless in order to help those that are unfortunate and to experience what it must feel like to be homeless. Whatever the reason, we can tell you that both are happy with what they have achieved and if, by chance, they meet each other, the bond either becomes inseparable or they could repel each other until the lessons they agreed upon before coming to Earth have been fulfilled.

Everyone has a twin flame. We may not get to meet them in this lifetime, but that does not mean that they are not out there. The vibration and the frequencies must match in order for you to come together.

Scribe: Is that the same as a soul mate?

Yes, a soul mate refers to someone you have known before in different incarnations; there could be a number of them. We call them soul groups as you have been together before in many past lifetimes, so therefore, resonate with each other or have the same attributes, vibration and familiarity.

> *What you see in someone is a perception that we carry with us that reflects a human essence that has accumulated over our existence.*

Unique

Live your life; you can't live anyone else's. We want to look and be a certain way, and it is all portrayed on social media. It is all fake news and false advertising to entice you to seek people who influence only themselves. Why follow celebrities who are fake from their head to their toes? You are unique in every single way, and you do not need to compete with anyone.

Your face is unique to you, and so is your body. We can enhance and reshape ourselves more healthily by eating right and exercising. Still, it is an insult to God when you reconstruct everything He gave you just to please society and the way you perceive yourself. It is a different situation if you were in an automobile accident and needed reconstructive surgery, but to deliberately maim yourself is dire. We have no judgement on what you choose to do with the body you have been given, but just know you are unique and perfect as you are!

Scribed by Nita Jane

Show the magnificence that you are.

Universal awareness

Fiction tells us stories are real; many are repeated over generations. When you think about the new generation, they are discovering these stories for the first time. There is one story in particular they haven't heard before that has the power to shape their entire worldview. What story? It is the story of the beginning of all mankind.

Older generations have awoken to this idea of learning and manipulating the minds of the young people with material written before. Whether it was positive or negative, the young have not lived it before, so they think it is something new and don't realise that the only reason it resonates with them is because they have lived it in a past life or experienced it too.

Whatever it is or was, they know it to be true because they feel it through their inner core. This millennium, people are drawn to mystics or religion because there is something within them that vibrates to that rhythm of knowing, which is the frequency from their past lives that they are beginning to remember and connect to. When there is familiarity around a conversation or an experience, for example, like déjà vu, the heart and soul know that this is not the first time it's been heard or seen.

Therefore, light switches start to ignite within, and you want to find out more about where you came from and who you really are. Some become dedicated to the cause, others learn and move on because they would have completed their journey with that particular experience. It is rare to have those who move to the beat of their own drum, like Leonardo da Vinci. Every single movement, thought, action, invention, writing, language, place, connection, person and building has always been here, only in a different time and space; we have only recreated it to suit ourselves.

Human beings can be categorised by what they are experiencing at this very moment. Some people go through sicknesses, abandonment, addiction, and the list goes on. How you deal with these afflictions determines how you will continue your life or not. Then the cycle starts, again and of course, you do not want to repeat that pattern of whatever it is. So, you learn from your situation and either make peace with your issues or deal with them through therapy and other means of self-development to help you cope through life. If you do not take action, it consumes and overwhelms you.

Life is very short, and what we do with it determines how we want to elevate ourselves once we go home and join the rest of the family that have passed. I doubt whether anyone wants to repeat an exam, for it could take up to many lifetimes to complete, and that is up to you. But take heed, the scenario will be the same as well as the situation, but the people will look different because you will have been reborn. How it plays out is anyone's guess, depending on the issue you never got to complete or get over.

Stories communicate the most wonderful visualisations that one can conjure up in their head. As human beings, you see the story and characters come alive the way you want them to. The storyteller and the receiver of the story work in unison with each other. The back-and-forth ritual of 'tell me more'. You do not need fancy paintings to know what you are looking at in your imagination. However, I myself prefer to look out at the environment around me and see through my own eyes, and write what I see. The celestial beings help me to see beyond the veil and show me their words of wisdom so I can write them down for everyone to read. I find myself intertwined with them all day, every day. I have learned everything from my higher self, which is my true self.

I am, in fact, blessed in all my life with wonderful family and friends, my purpose, health, nutritional food and the key that unlocks the stairway to the collective, universal truths.

I suggest you think about your situation right now and evaluate your life on earth. What have you learned? What do you want to learn? How is it going to affect you positively or negatively? You may not know until it hits you in the face, and sometimes it can be right under your nose. Know that you are loved. Do not ever think that you are alone. We can do this together in precious love for humanity. My love for you is eternal.

Let us clear and erase the cobwebs that tend to stifle us and cover our beautiful faces.

Universal energy

Your environment is changing, and so are you. The universal energy is lifting, and the vibration is too. We need stability in our lives right now. But we seem to fail at believing in ourselves. Rest assured that you are the best creation the Source has ever made. So do not think for a second that you are unworthy to walk this Earth. The sound of the universal trumpets rings in our ears, and you have only to listen and hear them.

They call you to accountability, for you are responsible for your own actions and what you are thinking. Be kind to yourself and start to control what you say to others. A loose tongue is an angry one, and there is no need for vulgarity. Life can be frustrating, we know. But that is placed in your path so that you may deal with it and overcome the challenges. You have guides with you; just know that. Ask and ye shall receive. We are eternally yours.

*Open your eyes. The world is
magical, and you are too.*

Validation

A compassionate mind will never be an angry one. You are a self-contained balancing unit without involving outside influences that you have in the past. Always push for validation from others, and when they say what they think, you are satisfied. Some of you live this way day-to-day through someone else validating your existence. Dear One, you have a direct link to God, and you do not have to be validated by anyone. You just need to know that God is within you, and that is good enough.

Dear One, it is I, Elohim.

Scribe: Welcome Dear Elohim.

I have come to remind you of your brilliance and love for mankind. Show your wisdom, Dear One. Speak your truth; do not be afraid to say how you feel. As the brook flows from the mighty mountain, so is the outpouring of love you will give to mankind. For we are the Source that also runs through you; you are the vessel that houses such energy. I see the raging waterfall as it cascades down, and now, I see the calmness it brings. Many people have their own war rising up inside of them. How to calm that war is where they seek someone like yourself to help instil the message of hope and perseverance and to continue their journey in life to fulfil their life purpose. Sometimes, the road is very long, but you will get there when you read the signs and listen to the almighty voice of the Lord.

*Why do you question the
magnificence within?*

Value

What do you value in your life? Is it your relationship with your children, family or spouse? Perhaps it is an animal that you raised from an early age. It could even be material possessions or money. Whatever it means to you, valuing something is an individual choice. The man with no shoes may value a new pair. A man who walks for miles may value a push bike. Spiritually, I value my awakening, for that has taught me to be truthful in all my encounters with situations and people in general, not only that I have a link with my guides, collectives and The Creator. Above all this is what I value. And, of course, my children, grandchildren and family, for they are the ones who physically, mentally, spiritually and emotionally support me when I am in need. Freedom arrives also when you value yourself most of all and when you become a mentor for others who may be lost. That is my personal encounter with values. Nothing material is valuable to me as I have no attachments to things that can be lost in a second or given away when it is time for me to leave the Earth.

What is it that you value most in life? Is it the material goods that cascade in your house so that it bulges at the seams? Or is it the love of your vehicle, the one you saved so hard to get? Whatever it is, this is personal to you. We have a habit of valuing material commodities rather than valuing our family and friends. Success can do strange things to people; those who supported you through the hard times no longer seem to matter. Of course, this does not apply to everyone. But I have seen this occur before on a number of occasions. Some become silent and go off the grid as they value their freedom. Some value the chance to protest their rights and the rights of others in order to live in a country that protects its people. We value the ground we stand on and the food that is grown for us to sustain ourselves. However, lately we have been destroying the forests and those animals that inhabit these rainforests.

So what do you think we should do about it? The government closes its ears and doesn't want to know. We've done all the protesting now; it is time to uplift the vibration and frequency of the new Earth, which has been foretold by many. As a collective with the right intention, we are able to lift the energy high enough to change the vibration. All in favour say, "Aye". I am forever in awe at the way the Universe works and brings people and places together. I am forever grateful and thankful to the celestial beings and Guardians that are always present in my life. If there have to be changes, God's Messengers will always be there to help mankind figure it out. We live in an unpredictable future where rules change on a daily basis, and we are left numb and confused by it all. There is a possibility that everything will work itself out and we will be back to normality (whatever that is). So hold on, folks, because we are all in for a bumpy ride.

You are more valuable than you think.

Vibration

As every year passes, we are facing a multitude of energy movements within human beings and the Earth. The shift is inevitable; it has been around for a while. The new age of awakening has just begun. More people are becoming spiritually engaged and learning new techniques to help them understand more about love and to change their ways accordingly. They are also mindful of the type of people they choose to connect with, which television shows to watch and choosing not to be so argumentative anymore, accepting people the way they are and not judging. This is going to become more of the norm now.

We are all going to ascend into five-dimensional vibration soon. It is affecting people physically, and the body has to start adjusting, but not too fast, for it could burn the body out entirely. Light beings are beginning to ascend to Earth in order to help humans adjust to their frequencies. We may not be able to see them, but they are here. Believe what you want to believe, but we are now in the era where it is time for the uprising of pure light to infiltrate the troubled Earth.

The darkness is beginning to fall away, and so are the dark lords that ruled the Earth. They will forcibly step down. More focus will be on the economics of each country and how we will work in unity rather than individually. After all, we are one race, the human race. Believe it or not, we are also a collective of connecting consciousness. We should be taking care of each other and refraining from corruption and political bullying.

The resources are for everyone to sustain their living conditions. There are many people out there who are very smart and know how to harness the natural resources, like the sun and wind, and generate electricity to run many towns. Technology is well-advanced, more so than what we have now, for the ETs know, and we need to be taught by them; there has been too much greed around. No one wants to share what they have learned, but that is a human trait. Not all are like this, but they are easily manipulated by money and sometimes threats. And so we wait.

How magical you are. You brighten the room with your zest for life and caring nature.

Vision

You see what you want to see in your everyday existence. To *really* see beyond the veil is truly amazing. As a child, I thought everyone could do this, but as I grew, I found that it is a very sought-after talent or gift, as many call it. To be able to see the spirits of those who have passed into the afterlife is, in fact, a natural ability that everyone has. I guess it is lying dormant in most and is waiting to be awakened. Awareness is referred to as those who have these abilities. I find it fascinating that we all have the same capabilities, and yet some are asleep to what they can do as human beings.

We question ourselves often, and we think other people are better than we are. The nonsense goes on, and the worst thing is you all start to believe it. Personally, I just want to be like everyone else, but that is not possible. I was awakened at birth and came from an extensive lineage of seers and healers. So now I embrace who I am and pass it on to the next generation. I now feel complete within myself.

> *You are the creator of your own design and your own perspective of the world around you.*

Water

The elixir of life, water, has memories within its droplets. It knows where it's come from and where it's going. Thank the water the next time you shower and cleanse your body while getting rid of debris that you have carried through the day. Thank the water as you drink, keeping your internal organs hydrated. Water is a magnet and acts like a compass; you will never be lost if you find a water source and follow the water upstream from where it flows. Salmon swim upstream to release their eggs. Why upstream? Because it is in their memory, as well as the memory of the water.

The Earth rotates around water, and without it, we would not exist. We spent nine months floating around in our mother's tummy, bringing us nutrients and life in water. We love to be near water because it reminds us of being in the womb. So the next time you sit beside a river, stream, or the ocean, close your eyes and listen to the sound of the water.

When you drink a glass of water, remember to think positive thoughts and acknowledge where the water is going, nourishing and sustaining your body and system. "Thank you again, beautiful water, for flushing the toxins from my body." We forget how important water is, and yet our bodies contain seventy per cent of it!

The life force of the water feeds the roots of the plants, which in turn nourishes the human being. We co-create on the Earth, and when we pass, our bodies go back to the earth and give back nutrients to the trees and plants. That is why we are part of the *all*; a never-ending recycling process, and what we do in between is up to us. We are to fulfil our purpose while on Earth. The Creator gave each and every one of us a gift. Find your gift; everyone has one. Otherwise you wouldn't be here.

*I thank you, precious water,
and I am grateful.*

Wisdom

Never be afraid to step forward into your light. Everyone has a light, and yours shines bright. It acts like a beacon on a stormy night, and others will follow your light, for they will see the wisdom that they seek. Many will want what you have, so become the way-shower for all. Wisdom of knowledge is all there for you, and healing is possible for everyone. All humans have a cellular system that repairs itself. Take control of your body awareness and acknowledge that it is there. You are starting to change within yourself, and you will have control over what you want in your life. Seek all that you need and want in your life. Help each other to understand what you are looking at. We as a society need to step up and encourage, support and change the way we currently do things. Great gifts have been given to all of humanity. Find them and use them; they are great tools to master.

> *"Knowing others is wisdom, knowing yourself is enlightenment."*
> – Lao Tzu

Work

Scribe: How are we going to better our lives when it comes to work?

Being more active with yourself and within the community. Volunteering will get you in a place of work-related jobs. There are also different avenues to be able to get where you are going or need to go. Life itself is to be experienced, to love, to show love and to experience love. Show others who you are. Take God's light with you wherever you go. Deal with the demons; get rid of them. Tune into the right frequency. How did you feel when you realised the money in your account is decreasing slowly?

Scribe: Feeling a strong sense of panic within the body. It is tingling from not knowing what the outcome will be if I don't do something very soon about employment. You could say I am worried about the future and where it's about to take me.

Fear not, for I am with thee. Close your eyes and envision the waterfall cascading in a rainbow of colours; they shimmer as they rest on the rocks. Life is like this, Dear One; life starts from the top and slides downhill, taking with it your troubles and woe. The significance of the water is like the life force which reaches the rocks below, and so too, Dear One, life as it explodes out in a million droplets while connecting to the earth. You have no idea where they have landed, but they have all dispersed themselves far away from the source. So you have to. You have forgotten that I am the Source, and you will need to make your way home over the treacherous rocks where you land.

Life is like this; we overcome barriers and obstacles on the way. My love for you is infinite as I watch and I wait. My Angels are there to help you conquer your fears and to bring you home. But first there are many trials you can undertake and many obstacles to overcome. We are here for you 100 per cent of the way. Patience, my lovely one; do not feel perturbed. Carry on with what you need to do in order for you to get where you're going.

Scribe: Redundancy is a situation no one wants to see themselves in. Ask the Divine guides, and they will help you find another. After asking for guidance, this is what came through from Spirit.

Nothing will come of it. Let go, and let us deal with it. There is always a reason you are taken out of employment. When you connect with your higher self, this is more important for your Earth mission. Everything is not by coincidence. All is done with precision and synchronicity, for we have made it so.

Trivial are your concerns, Dear One. We will take care of your circumstances.

With much trust in the Universe. The outcome was a new job on the two months after stressing and speaking to Spirit with Spirit. Now, that's a miracle in the making. It happens when you trust all is well.

Decide for yourself who you want to be.
The Universe is yours to take hold of.

Acknowledgments

Dear God, thank you for connecting me to the Source, knowledge of all knowledge, love of all love and all that there is.

I am grateful for many things in my life. First of all, my children, grandchildren and my family. I am grateful for my health. I am grateful for the food that nourishes my body. I am grateful that I am financially secure, always. I am grateful for the opportunities that have come my way and for accepting them.

I am especially grateful for the spiritual gifts that The Creator has given me.

To my sisters, MihiTerina, Evette, Elviena and Wilma, who put up with my constant barrage of questions. Thank you for supporting me throughout my journey and for giving me the courage to continue to pursue God's work, to persevere, and never give up.

To my brothers and sister in-laws, nieces and nephews and extended whanau, "Ka Nui Taku Aroha Ki a Koe." My love for you knows no boundaries.

To my children, Josephine, James, Nadja and Pauli. To my grandchildren, Shonnie, Joaquin, Manaia, Romeo, Jiani, Jasmine, James (JJ) and Aria, this book is for you, a legacy I leave behind to let you know anything is possible. If I can do it, so can you.

You are my forever blessings and the reason I wake up in the morning to greet the sun and walk upon the Earth. Thank you all for life's lessons. Arohanui

Scribed by Nita Jane

To my dear friend Janet, for answering all my endless questions about life and Spirit, and for your priceless friendship, guidance and precious wisdom.

To Reverend Barbara from the Aquarius Church and all the members. Thank you all for your welcoming, unconditional love.

To my dear friend Anne, what a treasure you are. Your infectious laughter still resonates with me. Thank you for believing in me.

About the author

I was told by a reader that I would be writing a book, but I never really imagined it would be something like this.

I am a mother, grandmother, sister and aunty. I am also the twelfth child in a family of fourteen. I am Tangata Whenua of Aotearoa (New Zealand) and Whakapapa (genealogy) to Ngāitai, Ngāti Kahungunu and Te Aitanga a Māhaki.

I was raised in a small timber town called Kawerau, where the primary income came from forestry.

From my earliest memories, connections with Spirit have always been as natural as breathing to me. I assumed this connection was natural for everyone. I vividly remember creating a painting at school and proudly showing the teacher the people in my artwork.

"People don't have purple faces and green arms," she scolded me.

I came home to tell my mother. She knew that I had the family gift and could see the coloured energy centres of the people around me.

"Stay quiet about this. No one outside the family needs to know," she said.

So, I kept quiet about my abilities and didn't explore them any further. It took many years for me to realise I had healing abilities as well as clairaudience and clairvoyance, allowing me to see and hear beyond the normal.

Scribed by Nita Jane

I fully embrace my gifts as a Reiki practitioner and connected spiritual being because these spiritual gifts, I believe, were handed down from my Tipuna (ancestors). As you know, the content of this book was channelled through The Creator.

I do not care to be famous. What I *do* want is for more human beings to know who they truly are. I hope the words you have read send a spark of hope to you so you will no longer stumble in the dark. Your quest for freedom is on the horizon; just a few more steps to go, my love, and you will be there. The shackles you made for yourself will fall away. Nothing will stop you from achieving your goals because you will finally find peace with yourself, embrace the new you, and walk your talk.

If you want to connect with me, please email NitaJane_08@outlook.com.au

Resources

If you have been triggered by any of the content in this book and need support, reach out to any of these resources for help.

Australia

Lifeline Australia, call 13 11 14 or visit www.lifeline.org.au.

Canada

Wellness Together Canada:
For youth, call 1-888-668-6810 or text WELLNESS to 686868.
For adults, call 1-866-585-0445 or text WELLNESS to 741741.
www.wellnesstogether.ca

New Zealand

Lifeline Aotearoa, call 0800 543 354 or visit www.lifeline.org.nz.

United Kingdom

Mind Infoline, call 0300 123 3393 or text 86463 www.mind.org.uk.

United States of America

Mental Health America, dial 988 or visit www.988lifeline.org.
You can also reach the Crisis Text Line by texting HOME to 741741.

International Mental Health Help Line Directory

If your country is not listed above, visit www.helpguide.org/find-help.htm to find the best contact point for you.

Milton Keynes UK
Ingram Content Group UK Ltd.
UKHW022019100524
442532UK00013B/371